A	B	C	D	E	F		

Eagles who Soar
how Black learners find the path to success

I	J	K	L	M	N	P	Q

SPECIAL NEEDS UNIT 01902 556256

Eagles who Soar
how Black learners find the path to success

Jasmine Rhamie

Trentham Books
Stoke on Trent, UK and Sterling, USA

Trentham Books Limited

Westview House   22883 Quicksilver Drive
734 London Road   Sterling
Oakhill   VA 20166-2012
Stoke on Trent   USA
Staffordshire
England ST4 5NP

First published 2007

British Library Cataloguing-in-Publication Data
A catalogue record for this book is available from the British Library

ISBN: 978 1 85856 394 7

Designed and typeset by Trentham Print Design Ltd, Chester and
printed in Great Britain by Cromwell Press Ltd, Trowbridge.

Contents

Acknowledgements

To undertake writing a book such as this does not come about as a result of the actions of one person. There were the individuals who contributed to the original research by taking time to complete questionnaires and were willing to be interviewed to share their experiences with me, I am so very thankful for their participation. I am indebted to Professor Susan Hallam at the Institute of Education who encouraged me to pursue this project and was consistent in her support, encouragement and advice. I wish to thank Gillian Klein for her wisdom and expertise in editing the numerous drafts of this book. I also thank the staff at Trentham Books. To my family, especially my children Serena and Jonathan who never failed to inspire and entertain me. And a special thanks to my friends who also encouraged me.

Finally, I must acknowledge the Creator God without whom I would not be here.

The research described in this book was made possible through the financial support of the Economic and Research Council (ESRC).

Dedicated to Serena and Jonathan

1

Introduction

The story is told of a farmer who placed an eagle's egg in the nest of a mother hen. When it hatched the baby eagle spent long summer days scratching around in the farmyard happily pecking for corn along with his adopted brothers and sisters.

One day a naturalist happened to visit the farm and was disturbed to see a beautiful eagle scratching around in the dirt with the chickens. He asked the farmer why the eagle was on the ground scratching and not soaring above the clouds, where the air is clear. The farmer shrugged and admitted that he didn't really know what to do with the bird.

With a determined air the naturalist picked up the flapping bird and placed it on the fence 'You are a beautiful eagle,' he declared, 'You are the king of the sky. You were not hatched to scratch around in the dirt but to soar above the mountain tops. Spread your wings and fly!' With that the naturalist gently pushed the bird off the fence. The eagle landed on the ground with a bump, ruffled its feathers and kept scratching around in the dirt.

Gritting his teeth the naturalist scooped the eagle up in his arms and held him aloft. 'O beautiful eagle, you are king of all birds, king of the sky,' he cried, 'You should not be scratching around in the dirt but soaring through the sky. Spread your wings and fly!' The naturalist threw the eagle into the air calling out for the bird to 'Fly! Fly!' The eagle fluttered its wings and shook its feathers and landed on the ground, scattering the chickens and proceeded to scratch and peck in the dirt.

The naturalist, now beside himself with grief, put the eagle in his van and drove to a nearby mountain. Clutching the bird in his arms he struggled to

climb to the summit. Sweating and panting he finally reached the mountain top. He carried the bird to the edge of the mountain. Holding it aloft, he shouted. 'You are an eagle, a magnificent bird! You are king of the sky! You were meant to soar above the clouds not scratch around in the dirt. Spread out your wings and fly! Fly! Fly!' And he launched the eagle over the edge watched anxiously as it appeared to falter, then it spread its vast wings and soared higher and higher above the clouds never to scratch in the dirt again!

Many Black children are scratching around in the dirt of school playgrounds in the UK. They were born to soar yet so many are failing to fly at school. For too long, the underachievement of Black children has been studied, re-searched, published and commented upon. Research papers focus on the depth and nature of the problem. Black children have been over-represented in the figures for exclusions, poor exam results, having Emotional and Behavioural difficulties (EBD), and receiving statements of Special Educational Need (SEN) Gillborn and Gipps, 1996; Osler *et al*, 2001 and Parsons *et al*, 2001). Lately, concern has focused on the poor performance of Black boys as they feature more than the girls in all these negative statistics. The constant emphasis on the underachieve-ment of Black pupils now overshadows those who do achieve. Despite the immense amount of research attainment figures for African Caribbeans have not improved significantly.

This emphasis on Black underachievement has resulted in Afri-can Caribbean children being labelled as educational under-achievers. Some researchers have challenged the concept of 'underachievement'. Coard (1971) and Tomlinson (1986) both considered it a problematic concept, its definition varying according to who was measuring it and for what purpose. The variety of definitions of underachievement range from those who equate it to scores on reading tests, Intelligence Quotient (IQ) tests and Standard Assessment Tests (SATs) to those who link it to the failure of acquiring particular qualifications or failing to achieve a university place.

Others challenge the legitimacy of making inter-group comparisons, questioning for instance, research concluding that Black pupils underachieve 'in relation to their peers' or 'in comparison to other groups' (Troyna, 1984). Such research assumes that comparisons are being made between two similar groups of children. However, the experiences of Black children in British society as a whole are fundamentally different to the experiences of White children or pupils from Asian backgrounds. These differential experiences affect pupils' motivation and attitudes to school and also teachers' and society's perceptions, which in turn have an impact on educational performance and achievement. Research which makes such comparisons without taking social factors into account is inevitably biased.

Gillborn (1990), for example, suggested that the term 'underachievement' is counter-productive as it implies that the problem is within the individual and ignores the possible influence of the education system. This has implications which negatively influence the way Black children are perceived and defined. It has been argued that it would be more accurate to conceptualise the current position of Black children in the UK in terms of 'educational disadvantage' or 'inequality' rather than 'underachievement' (Wright, 1988). Recently, however, there has been some progress: socioeconomic status, social class and gender are considered in recent research on ethnicity and education (see Gaine and George, 1999; Gillborn and Gipps, 1996; Gillborn and Mirza, 2000).

Also important is the sometimes biased and negative interpretations made from 'relatively slight evidence' (Taylor, 1981, p216). This has led to the proliferation of certain myths about Black people, their families and culture, which have muddied the waters in the search for solutions to the 'problem' of underachievement. In support of this view, Troyna (1984) asserts that the hopeless picture of Black underachievement at the time was not as clear as it appeared to be. He asserted that the 'distorted and grossly oversimplified empirical studies' (*ibid,* p154) have distracted educationalists and practitioners from addressing the real hindrances to Black achievement.

Research into the underachievement of ethnic minorities has slowed since 2000. There is now a growing interest in those who achieve academically. However, each year the government continues to publish statistics showing the ethnic breakdown of all groups of pupils taking General Certificate of Secondary education (GCSE) exams. These results continue to show African Caribbeans performing poorly compared to other ethnic groups (DfES, 2006).

After four decades of negative findings about the state of Black pupils' academic achievements it is time to shift the focus and redress the balance by researching the growing numbers of African Caribbeans who come through the British education system relatively unscathed. It is time to look more closely at the eagles who soar.

The purpose of this book is to raise the profile of high achieving African Caribbeans by sharing the results of a study undertaken to identify the factors which support their academic success. In addition, I hope it will enable us to celebrate the achievements of Black achievers in the UK.

The importance of the research for the educational futures of Black children in this country cannot be overstated. I have experienced first hand the British education system, as a pupil, then as a student, teacher and now teacher trainer and lecturer. I recognise the importance of investigating the experiences of my ethnic group, as we are suffering academically.

It is important that we now explore all aspects of African Caribbean children's learning: the pattern of underachievement, but also the factors that fracture that pattern and enable academic success. I hope the book will provide insight into the pupils' school and home experiences for the educators responsible for tackling achievement and school exclusions. Finally, I wish that *Eagles who Soar* will benefit the Black community itself and encourage its members to make greater efforts to improve the learning experiences of its children in Britain.

Origins of the study

The study presented here was inspired by the book *I am a Promise* by Yvonne Channer (1995). She interviewed twelve Black people who were succeeding scholastically and suggested that their success was a result of their involvement with and participation in Black churches. This raised the question, could encouraging involvement in Black churches be the answer to improving Black attainment? This seemed to me too simplistic an answer. Recalling my own church experiences, I could think of some in the church who had done very well but also people who had not. So I undertook a small scale study examining the experiences of fourteen academically successful Black men and women to establish the factors they deemed to have helped them achieve and to determine the extent to which the Black church contributed to their success (Rhamie and Hallam, 2002). These men and women were doctors, lawyers, academics, psychologists and so on or were currently completing postgraduate studies.

The results of that study revealed two models of success: the Home-Community model and the Home-School model. The first described the experiences of the majority of the group, showed the individual experiencing a 'sense of belonging', acceptance, achievement and success through the home and aspects of community life, including the Black church. These were people who were able to achieve despite attending a school where expectations were low and resources poor (Rhamie and Hallam, 2002). The second model described a continuous positive interaction between home and the school with both fostering excellence and success. The schools tended to be fee paying or grammar schools with overall high academic attainment. Pupils' homes and lifestyles were essentially middle class. Four of the fourteen individuals interviewed fit within this model.

So the question of the influence of the Black church turned out to be complex and I needed to investigate Black academic success further, this time using a larger sample and looking at the full range of attainment. I wanted to compare factors that contributed to high academic achievement, vocational achievement and underachievement, by considering other high achieving groups.

The essential question was this: why do some African Caribbeans succeed academically when the majority appear to be failing? What are the determining factors? I wanted to know whether there was something special or extraordinary about those who succeed. Or was it just that they came from wealthy Black families who could afford to pay for private education? I was interested in the individual factors as well as the environmental factors that differentiated high and low achieving African Caribbeans. Essentially, I wanted to know why eagles soar.

The study

During the year 2000-2001 questionnaires were distributed to a variety of venues such as local youth clubs, churches, community centres, employment and training centres. A number of Caribbean and African organisations were contacted, as well as the local Further Education College and the University. Parents from a local day nursery and delegates at a conference on Black issues were also approached and so were friends who in turn contacted their friends, so drawing in still more people. In the end 78 people returned completed questionnaires. They ranged in age from 16 to over 40; nearly two thirds (63%) were female.

The questionnaire sought information about employment, type of school attended, qualifications, and experiences at school including homework. It also explored parents' occupation, education, and attitude to education. There were also questions about out of school activities.

Some of those who completed the questionnaire indicated that they were willing to be interviewed to explore their responses further. A total of 32 Black people were interviewed for the study, half of them male and half female.

The research methodology aimed to enhance reliability and validity through triangulation of the interviews and the question-naires. Morse (1994) recommends thirty to fifty interviews for grounded theory studies to ensure validity. This was attained at the qualitative analysis level.

The study focused on exploring with Black adults their percep-tions and interpretations of their experiences in a range of con-texts at home, within the community and at school. I particularly focused on their personal stories of childhood and adolescence and their perceptions of what had contributed to their academic attainment. This was a phenomenological approach which values our perspectives of the experiences we have had. The theoretical basis of this approach lies within an ecosystemic framework influenced by grounded theory. This framework re-cognises that individuals interact within a range of systems such as the home, community and school which are themselves con-nected.

Bronfenbrenner (1979) emphasised the notion that development is influenced by human interactions within specific settings, the relationship between these settings and the larger context within which these settings are situated, and this further affirms my ap-proach.

Thus, this study looks at a range of social systems within which these individuals function. These social systems are the com-munity: formal and informal organisations, peer groups, role models, learning environments outside school such as supple-mentary schools, private tuition and music tuition. These sub-systems all affect the performance of children in schools. The other major social system outside the school is the home: not only parents but also siblings, relatives, routines and the physical home environment. The school is the other major ecosystem with which the child interacts the complex or simple interactions of individuals with others and the 'actions and reactions between participants' are significant (Upton and Cooper, 1991). The role of each ecosystem needs to be explored to come to an understanding of the influences at work.

From my analysis of the questionnaire and interview data I identified five groups of achievers. The British government's criterion for determining academic success at the end of secondary school (year 11) is to achieve at least five General Certificate of Secondary Education (GCSE) examination passes at grades A*-C. The successful groups were those who achieved at least the minimum 5 A*-C grades at GCSE and completed year 11 (the High Fliers), those who retook exams in the first few years after leaving school to eventually achieve at least 5 A*-C GCSEs (the Retakers) and those who returned to education as adults and achieved undergraduate and post graduate qualifications many years later (the Perseverers). People who had achieved only vocational qualifications were referred to as the Careerists. The final group were the Underachievers who mostly had no GCSEs or qualifications. Table 5.1 opposite shows the numbers of those participating in the study. (Note that the term success does not relate to the current status of those who participated in the study).

The High Fliers had broadly positive experiences across the home and community and although they had negative experiences in school they were better able to cope with them than members of the other groups. The Retakers also came from positive homes but received less practical support. Their negative school experiences seemed to affect them to some degree and their community experiences were slightly less consistent and involved than the High Fliers.

The Careerists came from homes where education was valued but parents lacked the necessary skills to support their children's

Table 5.1 Number of respondents in each group

	The High Fliers	The Retakers	The Careerists	The Underachievers	The Perseverers	Total
Questionnaires returned	37%(29)	13%(10)	14%(11)	18%(14)	18%(14)	78
Interviewees	41%(13)	16%(5)	9%(3)	16%(5)	19%(6)	32

education. Experiences across the community and school were less inconsistent and positive. The Underachievers' experiences contrasted to those of the High Fliers. Home, school and community experiences were mainly negative and were characterised by high levels of problems and difficulties.

The Perseverers had mixed experiences across the home, school and community. While they valued education, they received little practical help, school was largely a negative experience and community involvement ranged from positive and active to negative and inconsistent.

Four themes emerged: Home, Individual, Community and School. This book looks in detail at the experiences of the five groups and the factors that played a part in their achievements. The experiences of African Caribbeans are presented in their own words. All names and locations have been changed to protect confidentiality.

Structure of the book

Chapter one introduces the book and the origins of the study. Chapter two attempts to explain why eagles soar. It seeks to identify what makes the difference between success and failure at school and applies the medical concept of resilience to education. It explains the relevance of resilience in education to school success.

Chapters three to seven describe in detail the experiences of each group of achievers in turn – the High Fliers, Retakers, the Perseverers, the Careerists, and the Underachievers – using the data from the questionnaires and interviews. Parents and families are placed under scrutiny: their relationships, support with homework, and parents' attitudes and expectations. Individual characteristics are examined such as motivation and the goals or personal challenges which hindered or aided progress. The experiences in the community are also explored, such as church attendance, music tuition, sport and youth clubs and use of libraries and museums. Also considered are school experience: the school ethos, attitudes to school, the teachers and the quality of teaching.

Chapter eight discusses the findings and considers some limitations of the study. The book concludes with recommendations for all those involved in the education Black children.

2

Why do Eagles Soar?

The research described in this book sought to explore the experiences of Black learners. It is based on the phenomenological accounts of adults' experiences and interactions within the ecosystems of school, home and community as well as considering individual factors. That is, adults reflecting on their school years and sharing their experiences and the factors they deem to have supported their academic achievement. I sought to identify the factors which support success and to explore these within the ecosystems of the individual. The analysis of the questionnaire and interview data provides a clearer picture of the educational experiences and influences at work in the lives of the Black learners who took part in this study.

The key research questions were: What are the factors that influence some Black learners to succeed academically when the majority appear to be underachieving? What are the individual and environmental factors that differentiate high achieving and low achieving Black learners? Are the effects of school exclusion and low attainment at the end of secondary school damaging to their academic attainment in the longer term?

The factors contributing to academic success are considered in chapter three in relation to the High Fliers and their experiences within each ecosystem. It highlights the cumulative effect of positive factors in each of the ecosystems which work towards their success.

The following chapters describe the characteristics of each group which indicate the differences in their home, school and community environments. These chapters therefore address the second question: the individual and environmental differences between the groups.

Finally, the disadvantages of low attainment did not affect all Black learners in the same way. Some returned to education and others did not. This book supports the anecdotal evidence that most Black children face negative experiences at school as this was found to be true for all the groups of every level of attainment. These negative experiences include some or all of the following: lack of support and encouragement from some teachers, a sense of being treated differently from their White peers, being subject to racism or having difficulties with teachers and other pupils. In addition, some were prevented from taking higher status examinations or those which would allow them to achieve at least a C grade in GCSE. These are common experiences that vary in intensity, scope and frequency. What is crucial is that these negative school experiences do not affect all children in the same way. The difference between those who are negatively affected and those who are not lies, I believe, in certain protective factors that give the children resilience to negative experiences. These protective factors develop through the positive interaction and influence of the ecosystems of home, community, individual and school.

The negative experiences Black learners have at school may arise from interactions with teachers and staff which leave them feeling that they have been treated differently or unfairly compared to other children. They also find a general lack of support and encouragement from teachers as well as negative, sometimes racist interaction with other children. My research participants reported experiences of this kind, familiar from decades of documentation.

Racism as a factor contributing to differential attainment levels has been well documented and cannot be ignored. The issue of racism was identified by Rampton (1981) but fudged in the final report into the differential achievement among ethnic groups under Swann (1985). Only when Macpherson (1999) identified institutional racism within education in the inquiry into the death of Stephen Lawrence was there wider recognition of the reality.

Gillborn and Youdell (2000) highlight the influence of league tables which have produced an A*-C economy in which schools are judged on the proportion of pupils achieving A*-C grades at GCSE level. This inevitably leads to minority ethnic pupils being discriminated against and perceived as failures. There is also evidence of the Black boys in school particularly facing high levels of conflict situations with teachers (Majors, 2001; Sewell, 1997; Wrench and Hassan, 1996). Other evidence of racism in schools can be found in Majors (2001), Gillborn (2001 and 2002), Crozier (2001) and Gillborn and Mirza (2000).

That the Macpherson Report (1999) implicated schools as being institutionally racist was acknowledged by many as a positive step which placed racism on the political agenda. But arguably the opportunity for bringing about real change in the area of race equality was missed as the government submerged and diluted key issues of race discrimination under the policy of social inclusion (Gillborn, 2001).

Ofsted published a report highlighting the lack of effective, clear strategies in many Local Education Authorities (LEAs) and schools for tackling racism and raising the attainment of ethnic minority pupils (Ofsted, 1999). Consequently, schools and LEAs were required to set out specific targets and plans for improving the performance of ethnic minorities. Follow-up research by

Ofsted found improvements in LEA and school support for ethnic minority pupils' attainment but that there was wide variation between LEAs (Ofsted, 2001a). It made recommendations for more sustained and effective plans and action in addressing the needs of ethnic minority pupils.

Given overwhelming evidence of racism in schools and the negative challenges faced by Black pupils, what is it that enables some to achieve against the odds? I believe the difference between those who are successful academically and those who are not lies largely in the cumulative effect of positive experiences at home where parents have high expectations, are encouraging and provide practical help with homework. Those who are High Fliers also benefit from the cumulative effect of positive experiences within the community where activities are achievement oriented, regular and consistent, voluntary and enjoyable. These positive effects help to build children's resilience and this enables them to process negative experiences in ways that do not distract from their goals.

Withstanding the ongoing impact of low school attainment and school exclusion is dependent upon the resilience children develop through home and community experiences. If these have been negative it may be difficult for resilience to develop. Positive interaction between the ecosystems of home, community and school is crucial in ensuring the highest possible academic outcomes for Black children.

Resilience

This book starts from an acknowledgement that most Black children have had some negative experiences at school. We saw that research into schools and their impact on Black children reveals evidence of racism at various levels which negatively affected children and their progress through school. Ask most Black parents and they will recount experiences of negative encounters between their children and teachers or other pupils. I recently

conducted a workshop where Black parents shared their frus-
trations and pain over teachers' lack of belief in Black children
and their tendency to make stereotypical negative assumptions
about their lives and capabilities. Successful children are those
who learn to navigate through these negatives and minimise
their impact. They are able to do so because they come from
strong, supportive homes with high expectations and are actively
involved in challenging but supportive community activities. The
positive influence of parents and the support of the community,
particularly the Black church, enable success. Positive support
engenders resilience which helps children to counteract the
negative impact of school experiences. It is the interaction between the home and community which provides children with
what they need to succeed in school. If the school also provides a
strong and supportive achievement oriented environment,
success is even more likely.

The unsuccessful children are those whose home and community experiences are less positive. They are given little practical help and support. There may be problems at home and
involvement in the community is inconsistent and not strongly
supportive. As a result these children are more vulnerable and
susceptible to the detrimental impact of negative school experiences.

The children who succeed after leaving formal schooling, sometimes years later, such as the Retakers (chapter four) and the Perseverers (chapter five), are aware of their parents' positive
attitude towards education and high expectations and recognise
its importance and value. But they were insufficiently resilient to
withstand the impact of negative experiences at school. Their
parents' low level of education may also contribute, if it prevented them from giving practical help and support. Although
some members of these groups were active in the community
they did not receive strong enough support to protect them
against negative factors, perhaps because of inconsistency or a

lack of commitment and engagement. They are less protected, so more vulnerable to the negative experiences encountered in school and fail to achieve academically. But the effect of their experience may not necessarily last all that long. The sense that education is valued plus their parents' positive attitudes and encouragement may be factors in their continuing pursuit of qualifications after compulsory schooling.

The concept of resilience originates in the field of psychiatric risk research and considers risk and protective factors which can assist in understanding how, for example, the individuals in this book were able to achieve despite the negative impact of school (Rutter, 1987). Resilience can be defined as the ability to recover from hardship because of protective factors. It is not a static characteristic. It is variable, dependent upon the individual and the particular risks being faced (p317). So one might be resilient at school and achieve success but the protective factors that ensure success might then be less effective in another adverse situation. Risk factors for Black pupils would be negative school experiences, the low educational attainment of parents and their employment in low level occupations, and problems at home. Protective factors have been shown to be positive interactions with parents and support at home, high expectations, positive and constructive interactions, and consistent, positive activities within the community (Richman and Bowen, 1997). The nature of risk and protective factors is also dependent upon the socio-cultural context of development and may not be the same for everyone (Haight, 2002). Other researchers have described protective factors in terms of providing a buffer against adverse stresses encountered and suggest that it is the individual, and factors within families and communities which mediate against adverse circumstances (Pollard, 1989).

Research, particularly in the USA, has found that the religious practices of African-Americans promote the development of protective factors, which create resilience, in children who face the harsh realities of racism, poverty and disadvantage (Haight, 2002). This book suggests that resilience is developed as a result of positive relationships with adults and consistent, constructive, supportive interactions at home and in the community – which may include church attendance and involvement. It is this resilience that needs to be developed in Black children to ensure success not just at school but throughout their careers.

Parental involvement in education and the home environment was certainly important to the achievement of the Black learners described in this book. Studies of the role of parental involvement in general have found it so positive that it is a feature of government documentation to schools (DfEE, 2000). The High Fliers had home environments conducive to completing homework and received the most help with homework from their families. This significant finding suggests that all parents would benefit from guidance and support on how they can help their children with homework.

Other research in this area has found that the parents of successful children showed an interest in their child's work and actively promoted work in the home encouraging reading and writing. They were also in regular contact with schools (Nehaul, 1996). Tomlin (2006) studied successful primary and secondary pupils and Osler (1997b) studied ten successful Black teachers: both found parental involvement a crucial factor in success. A number of home factors contribute to developing resilience which in turn contributes to success: positive support and encouragement from parents; a structured home environment; practical help with homework; and high expectations (Gillborn and Gipps, 1996; Lee, Winfield and Wilson, 1991; Nehaul, 1996; Rhamie and Hallam, 2002; Tomlinson, 1983). This evidence refutes the stereotyped perception that Black children fail because their parents are uninterested in their schooling (see Crozier, 1996; Tizard, *et al* 1988; Wright, 1992).

Expectations

A key factor in academic success is the impact of parents' expectations on children's achievements. Rhamie and Hallam (2002) found that the most successful Black learners reported that their parents had high expectations of them. Parents expected them to do well. Failure was not an option. Thus, going to university and succeeding in examinations was regarded as a normal part of their progress through life. This study of academically successful Black learners found that parents were clear in transmitting their expectations of their children to do well at school and achieve high grades.

Parents of the High Fliers were employed in higher occupational levels than the other groups. It has been well documented that parent occupational levels are associated with school attainment. Mackinnon *et al* (1995) found that the children of professionals were over ten times more likely to go into higher education than those of unskilled manual workers. Owen *et al* (2000), in a review of statistical data on education, training and the labour market, found that students of all ethnic groups with fathers in managerial or professional positions were nearly twice as likely to achieve 5 GCSEs at A*-C grades as students with a father in a manual occupation. However, there is evidence that Black pupils who have high social class status still suffer inequalities in educational attainment (Gillborn and Mirza, 2000).

Rhamie and Hallam (2002) also found a correlation between parental education and pupils' academic achievement. Some parents with poor levels of education nonetheless had high aspirations for their children and encouraged them to work hard at school. There was also evidence that despite their own poor education parents knew the value of education as a route out of poverty and disadvantage. And although they lacked the skills or tools to assist with school work at home, their positive encouragement and verbal support was instrumental in their children's subsequent academic success.

This is supported by research on disadvantaged families which found high levels of parental involvement which included parents and children engaging in discussion in the home lives of successful Black students (Yan, 1999). This suggests that success is possible among all social classes.

The High Fliers' parents were generally critical of the education system and sought to question and closely monitor their children's progress through it. Research on academically successful Black learners also found that parents did not trust schools and took specific measures to support their child's progress, for example, not allowing their children to be pushed into sporting activities at the expense of academic work (Rhamie and Hallam, 2002). Black parents' lack of trust in the school system has been supported by other research conducted by Yan (1999) and Crozier (2001). Overall, the role of parents and home factors is highly significant in supporting the positive academic experiences of Black learners.

The impact of the community on the academic lives of Black learners has to be seen in conjunction with additional protective factors within the individual and the home. There is considerable value in active and committed involvement in community activities. The academically successful were involved with community activities in combination with other positive factors in the other ecosystems in their lives, which provided protection from the adverse impact of the negative experiences they had at school and the challenges faced through navigating the barriers imposed by race and social class. These Black children were able, because of the strength of resilience developed through the home and community, to resist negative pressures at school and achieve success.

Within the community, the Black church provides opportunities for positive, confidence building interactions and experiences. The benefits of being actively involved in church life were explicitly reported. Church involvement provides a system of support for parents and children, which has implications for dealing with life in an often impoverished, unwelcoming environment where they may not feel accepted. However, if the experience of church attendance is negative or attendance imposed, this weakens the potential benefits. In 1997, it was reported that 57 per cent of Black people attended Black churches in the UK (Modood, *et al* 1997), implying that the influence of the church is important in their lives. More recently, the 2005 English Church Census found that Black church attendance is at least three times their proportion in the population and has increased by over 19 per cent since 1998. Furthermore 85 per cent of ethnic minority attendance has been in ethnic minority congregations (Brierley, 2006) and 85 per cent of Black young people reported that they believe in God (*The Black Child Report*, 2000). This is important as religious belief has been found to be significant in the lives of successful Black pupils (Channer, 1995; Rhamie and Hallam, 2002). In a study of African American children in church, Haight (2002) found that children's spiritual belief systems, socialisation and participation in the child centred activities of the church contributed to their resilience.

The Black community provides opportunities for children to use their time and resources to participate in constructive activities which enable them to acquire and reinforce their skills (Nettles, 1991). However, this involvement needs to be active and committed, as evidence from the achievement groups indicates that the community experiences of the successful groups were not only positive and enjoyable but also consistent. The more negative, irregular pattern of involvement found in the low achieving groups seems to have lessened the positive effects of community involvement. Positive involvement combined with a supportive home environment develops self esteem and self efficacy – protective factors that can help young people resist and overcome negative influences in school.

The positive influence of the home and community contributes to a sense of belonging – a theme which has featured in other research on Black academic success. Channer's (1995) respondents stressed the importance of being cared for and valued by their families and community. The Black teachers in Osler's (1997c) study described the sense of belonging arising from being part of 'a very secure community' (*ibid*, p.119). Respondents in other studies described the positive and supportive environment of home and community as providing a strong network for the child (Rhamie and Hallam, 2002). When both home and community are supportive they provide children with protective factors and a feeling of security. They know that they belong and have a sense of place which is an essential part of ethnic identity (Rampton, 1995), and this aids resilience.

Having personal goals was a key determinant for the High Fliers. Goals included a desire to do well, to attend university, pass examinations, and enter high level careers. Rhamie and Hallam's research on Black success (2002) found similar themes of self-motivation and confidence in goal orientation. That the accounts of the other groups showed that they did not have goals when at school suggests that having a purpose is important. It helps to motivate pupils and focuses their attention on completing the tasks, which are necessary steps towards achieving their goals.

Other mediating factors in individuals also affect resilience, for instance, aspects of intrinsic motivation, self-perception and attitudes (Hildago *et al*, 1995). Many of those who succeeded described being well motivated and desired to achieve. For some this motivation was driven by their parents' influence and motivation for them to succeed. In her observations of successful pupils, Nehaul (1996) found that a number of influences were working towards pupils' success and named confidence, task application and motivation among others. Much motivation has been linked to self esteem and self efficacy. An individual's belief about themselves and their capabilities to organise and act in order to attain their goals is essential in motivating them to acquire the skills they need to complete tasks (Shunck, 1987). Parents' belief in their children promoted the development of self belief, and self motivation in the successful learners and was an important influence in their achievements.

There were significant differences in the age range of the five groups I identified. The High Fliers were mainly comprised of the youngest of the sample aged between 16 and 25 whereas the others were mostly over thirty. This suggests that educational opportunity for Black children has improved in recent years so that more of the younger respondents achieved five GCSE exam passes. It may also indicate an improvement in the strategies used by these students to navigate the British educational system. Many of their parents would have been through the school system themselves but this is surmise. Actual reasons remain unclear. But GCSE examination results for 2006 indicate that Black pupils are still the lowest performing ethnic group, with 47.5 per cent achieving 5 GCSEs at the end of secondary school. The results indicate that Black pupils have fallen below Bangladeshi and Pakistani pupils and are now the lowest performing of all groups with the exception of Travellers of Irish Heritage and Gypsy/Roma, which are far smaller groups (DfES, 2006).

The majority of the sample was female, with the exception of the Perseverers, which was predominately male. Reasons for this may interface with Sewell's research into Black youth culture and its influence on school achievement (2000) or indeed with disproportionate numbers of Black boys being excluded from school and so having their education disrupted. Black males consequently take longer to achieve educationally. Although it is encouraging that the male respondents in this group had achieved academically, this finding presents the education system with a challenge to examine its policies and procedures for dealing with Black pupils, particularly boys, and to ensure that they are able to access the system fully so they can achieve whilst still in compulsory education.

Schools have responsibility for educating Black pupils, like all pupils, to achieve their full potential. My research reveals some of the failings of teachers and schools to fulfil their responsibilities towards these pupils. Black learners in the study also drew attention to the question of why certain teachers relate to Black pupils differently from White. If high expectations of Black pupils become the norm for teachers this will influence the expectations Black pupils have of themselves, improve their feelings about school and create positive environments where high achievement can flourish.

My study found excluded pupils in all achievement groups, indicating that all pupils are susceptible to exclusion, regardless of academic ability. This suggests that exclusion is less an indicator of problematic behaviour in a particular child and more a reflection of the failure of schools to deal adequately and fairly with conflictual situations, particularly those arising from racial harassment (Blair, 1994; Gillborn and Youdell, 2000; Ofsted, 1996).

A high incidence of school exclusion was evident. School exclusion is the removal of a pupil from school permanently or temporarily due to breaking school rules. The accounts of exclusion point to injustices in the system. Whilst there were some who felt that their exclusion was justified, a number of those interviewed did not. A picture emerged of pupils being punished without their side of the story being heard. This led to feelings of injustice. There was no resentment about being punished for wrongdoing; indeed they accepted that sanctions should be imposed for wrongdoing. There was a strong sense of dissatisfaction felt by those involved because of the differential treatment they experienced. There is a case to be answered as to whether exclusions of Black pupils are always justifiable.

Many Black children face the challenge of low social class status and the economic burdens their parents, families and communities have to deal with. They also encounter the challenge of being Black in a predominantly White society. This leaves them having to cope with negotiating their way through a complex, ambiguous and sometimes hostile world, where the messages they absorb about themselves are not always positive. It is within this climate that Black children need to develop resilience in order to succeed. Resilience is strengthened through active support in the home, as well as supportive and achievement oriented, culture enhancing, character and confidence building community endeavours. The school system must continue to work towards providing safe, secure, accepting, achievement focused learning environments that will ensure all pupils have optimal opportunities to succeed.

3

Eagles who Soar:
The High Fliers

The High Fliers achieved at least 5 GCSE A*- C grades or equivalent at the end of secondary school. Most were aged between 16 and 25. The other achievement groups were mainly composed of people over thirty. The High Fliers had the youngest age profile of all. They made up 37 per cent (29) of the whole sample and were the largest group to return questionnaires. Thirteen were interviewed. Although more women responded to the study overall, the High Fliers had similar proportions of men and women. Forty one per cent were employed in professional occupations, fewer than for the Retakers, and 28 per cent were full time students. All were employed, none of them in manual occupations.

At home
Education valued by parents
The members of the High Fliers characteristically came from homes where education was valued. Parents were described as giving explicit verbal messages to their children about the importance of education. Some remembered these messages verbatim:

Oh my goodness! They used to say to me 'Education is the key to success! (Barbara)

...The most important thing my dad always said 'You know, they can't take it [education] away from you, so you need to learn and I don't care what they are trying to do to you, just ignore that and get your qualification because it's yours at the end. They cannot take it away from you.' And he couldn't stress that enough. (Charlene)

That education mattered to the parents was clearly communicated to their children, who wanted to please parents by succeeding. This wanting to please developed into a determination to do well.

They were behind me; they were behind me 100 per cent. I felt that and I knew that if I failed the school wouldn't much matter and my peers wouldn't much matter, but my parents were all important. Just to succeed and do well at school and that I understood and I realised that commitment and I wasn't going to falter on that for them and myself. (Glen)

Practical help

Not only were parents positive about education but they also gave practical help and support as well as verbal encouragement. The practical help and support took the following forms: a set routine at home with homework as part of this routine; receiving the most help of all the groups with homework particularly from parents and family members. Parents were actively involved in their learning experience.

Ninety two per cent reported having support from parents, the highest of all the groups.

They have been very supportive in that they would help with revision and things. Like I would do questions and things and my mum would mark them and help me set up a timetable, lots of practical things. (Marvin)

I remember my dad, since we were around 5 he would show us the clock and he was making sure we knew the time. He helped us to

> spell and we were always encouraged to read. My mum reads and she used to write you know so there was a lot of that around and they definitely encouraged us too, both of them equally. (Charlene)

One student had paid tutors who were brought in to help prepare her for A-levels. Parents assisted with revision and in purchasing workbooks for their children to do extra work.

Not only were the parents generally better educated than those of the other groups but over half the mothers were employed in managerial or professional occupations and so were 37 per cent of fathers. The few parents who did not have the educational background or high status occupations still did their best to support and encourage their children.

> Just like anybody her age and with her background [she believed you must] make full use of education. Because obviously she didn't want me to become a cleaner, you know, like she was. She wanted me to be educated so I could go further than that. She wasn't able to complete her education, but she valued it. (Trent)

> Well, I think they knew they might not know all that I needed to put into getting the right grades. But they knew about A B C D, that was pretty self-explanatory to them. So they knew that if you said D it wasn't good, but if you said A it was good. They didn't necessarily know all that you needed to put into improving how to get from a C to an A, but they understood that much. I suppose they were always encouraging in terms of 'Well you know you need to try harder and you need to try better next time'. You know often words were not used to encourage but you knew they wanted you to do well. (Glen)

Parents used a range of supportive measures to supplement their children's formal education. Others gave positive encouragement and stressed the importance of education.

Family expectations were made explicit by some, while others left it unspoken. But it was clearly understood:

> I knew I had to do it because I was expected to go to school. After that I would go to university. It is like an expectation that my family had. So I knew I had to go through that. (Barbara)

> If there were problems there [at school] I wasn't necessarily caught up in them and I suppose it was still a case of if there were you're still going to succeed at school. And even if there was racism you were going to succeed and I suppose that came from the family really. This thing about succeeding, doing well at school, whatever and I was able to sort of concentrate and get on and I was given the freedom to do that. (Glen)

The High Fliers valued their parents' efforts and recognised that even those who were not well educated had high expectations of them academically. It was made clear that being educated and qualified was not an option but a necessity. The accounts by the group gave an indication of the significant role parents' expectations play in encouraging achievement. Some of the Retakers reported similar parental expectations and encouragement, but was not in evidence in the other achievement groups.

The families of the High Fliers were regarded by the participants as providing motivation for them to do well. It was this motivation and drive from the family that helped to maintain a focus on achieving their goals. Some who did not specifically mention the family as motivating grew up in homes where older siblings attended university. Almost two thirds of the group reported having motivators within their families.

> But I could be motivated you see, my dad tended to motivate me... I think what my dad was saying was if you don't have a job or if you are doing a job if you can get qualified, then you can get more money. So I was motivated by the fact that if I can get the qualifications, then I'm in a better position careerwise... (Charlene)

Encouragement, support and having motivators within the family contributed to the achievements of this group.

Homework and routines

Homework is a major part of every pupil's learning. How this takes place in the home, with or without parents' involvement often reveals the value parents place on education. Most of the members of this group had help with homework. Parents were, to varying degrees, involved in the completion of homework and considered it an important part of their child's education.

> I suppose, the way mum and dad are that they put it in our heads, that we've just got to learn to do our homework. My mum would switch the telly off when we got in from school and we just had to do our homework. There were no questions asked until it was done. (Jolene). There was an expectation whether my parents were there or not that the homework had to be done. (Barbara)

Completion of homework often defined the routine after school.

> We had quite a strong disciplined time schedule, in that we all had a personal chore. Mine was sweeping the stairs and so when I came home from school, before I did anything I had to sweep the stairs. But it was something like do your chores, then you wash your face, and have dinner, worship then homework something like that. That was very regular, very consistent. (Aaron)

Parents did more than instructing their children to complete their homework: they constructively checked and monitored it.

> In secondary school it was my mum, mostly. But she didn't help that much, I tended to do that myself. The help I got from my mum was reminding me to do it, but occasionally like glancing at me to see what I was doing and giving me a hand if I was stuck. (Joshua).

In short, the parents of the High Fliers were aware of the importance of homework. They encouraged a set routine, which allocated time for homework and constructively encouraged their children to do it.

> Well, my dad, he was very keen he would help me with my school work. He was very keen to get involved and see what was happening... When I was like doing the 11 plus, he would get the books for me, and that continued into secondary school... Yes, I remember doing a lot of extra work myself. (Neville)

> I know when I was going to primary school I used to have to come home in the evening and read. My dad used to make me read. I don't know how old I was at that time. And I think there was like, sometimes

holidays when they would buy the workbooks and stuff and my mum used to make us do some of those as well. (Simon).

Homework as part of the evening routine characterised the lives of the High Fliers, although it was not always parents who provided help with homework. Whilst over half did receive help from parents, help often came from other sources such as relatives, older siblings and friends. Statistical analysis of the questionnaire data found that there was a significant relationship between receiving help with homework during primary and secondary school and achieving at least five GCSE A*-C passes. Over 70 per cent had help with homework during secondary school and 76 per cent during primary school.

Distrust of the school system

A higher percentage of the High Fliers' parents than the others were reported to distrust the education system. Some High Fliers reported that parents checked the progress of their children closely because they expected the school to deny full educational rights to their children in some way. They had believed at first that the school would do the best for their children but various experiences turned their trust to distrust and they realised that the progress of their children in school would require close monitoring.

Barbara described how her parents attended parents' evening for the first time when she was in year 10 and discovered that although school reports had indicated that she was 'doing well' the highest GCSE grade she could get in her maths was a D. This made her parents work harder so they could provide extra tuition at home and they encouraged her to show her teachers that she had the ability to achieve a higher grade. Barbara consequently improved and was moved up through the ability groups.

Another parent, after an incident with his older son being kicked by a teacher in school, recognised that he needed to monitor the school.

But then he became aware that he needed to keep an eye on schools here, because before he just thought, 'Oh, the children are misbehaving, so of course the teacher would hit them'. But he didn't understand that they were hitting them because they were Black... So it was from that really that he realised that he needed to keep a check. If he wanted the children to get an education here, with all the situation with the racism, he needed to keep a check on the school. (Charlene)

Close attention to what was happening with the education of their children at school was important for the respondents' success, even if it was precipitated by negative experiences.

Individual characteristics

Members of the High Fliers described a number of individual characteristics which influenced their attainment: motivation, religious belief and goals. They were the only group who referred to having goals while at school.

Motivation

Motivation was described as originating from a range of sources such as religious belief, determination and competition. Other elements included self-determination, having personal goals, and having significant individuals including parents, friends, and teachers who were a source of motivation. Experiencing challenges which encompassed anything the individual saw as potentially threatening and wanted to overcome might motivate them too, such as racism, unfair treatment, or being naturally competitive. Some described their motivation as deriving from within themselves through qualities such as being focused and determined, self-disciplined and hardworking and having high self esteem and ambition, having a positive outlook or being independent. They liked to do well.

Over three quarters of the group described themselves as having such personal characteristics:

...I knew the things that interested me and I knew the things that I wanted to do. I know I am the only person who can make them happen, in the sense that if I don't do the things I need to do, if I don't do the work and put in the time and the effort it's not going to happen. Nobody can make it happen for me. I can't expect other people to make it happen for me either. And I'm kind of pretty independent and I like to do things for myself. (Jadanna)

Self-motivation was evident, as was the recognition that achievements are accomplished through personal effort. A natural desire to do well, to accomplish tasks, and to learn from those around him was the formula for success for Simon:

I suppose I'm the type of person that likes to do well. If I set out to do something I like to at least achieve or at least gain something from doing it. So if I put time into it then I actually get something out of it. And probably when you see how you learn from other people as well, when you see how well someone's done then you can learn some methods from that.

Along with their internal motivational drive, some respondents in this group were driven by competition. When asked what motivated him, Joshua replied,

Probably my cousin, the year before he took his GCSEs and he got a few fails and I wanted to beat him. More the competition, I have always been competitive.

I felt that I was motivated because I wanted to be. I think we were very competitive at school, as well. Certainly, in our year, with KC and all those people and we always used to push to be the top of the class. (Trent)

Religious belief
Religious belief including regular study of the Bible, prayer and faith in God were specific factors perceived by the High Fliers to have contributed to their success.

I think the church can provide something additional as well that the school can't provide... (Glen).

Trent attributed his success to a combination of factors including religion:

> ... I think a combination of the emphasis on the relationship with God, doing well at school, pursuing your goals, your dreams. That emphasis from both church and school and class with the support that I got from my mum I think did it for me and what contributed to me I think is working and working hard. (Trent)

Religious belief as a factor in academic success was mentioned by 31 per cent of this group. The tenets of religion appear to have served as an underlying support for their motivation to achieve.

Goals

One characteristic unique to the High Fliers was having goals. Over half mentioned personal goals. The people who were successful knew what was needed for academic success from an early age. They clearly knew where they wanted to go. Not all were sure what career they wanted to enter, nor the degree they wanted to do or even if they wanted to go to university. But all wanted to do well.

> I think I am one of these people. I mean throughout my life I had a very clear idea of what I wanted to be. (Charlene).

> I didn't do as well as I should have in fifth year. I did want to pick up a bit and I did have the aim of wanting to continue further studies. (Neville)

The younger respondents in this group were clear about the next step and made statements such as:

> I intend to go to university maybe law but I am not sure. (Joshua)

> Next year I will be finalising plans for going to university. And I will take my A-level final exams next year. (Marvin).

> Medicine is something I've always wanted to do. (Fiona)

Thus we see the High Fliers describing their goals in various terms while being clear about where they were heading and what they hoped to achieve.

Individual problems and difficulties

Overall, few problems were identified by the High Fliers. The only ones related to failing exams. One participant indicated that laziness played its part in their approach to some subjects and another mentioned being distracted by peers. In response to the question, 'What reasons would you give for not passing all of your exams?' Joshua said:

> Due to my own laziness but the teachers like would warn me like do your course work sort of thing and I would say like yeah I'll do it. Got a bit caught up with all of it. But I got off, passed – with some As. But I was just lazy.

Community

The study explored the activities pursued by these pupils when they were not in school. These included attendance at church and its clubs, music tuition, youth clubs, sports and visits to libraries and museums. Their accounts of engagement in such activities were more positive than for other groups. The community was a source of motivators, encouraging friendships and role models. Their involvement was broadly positive, voluntary, active and consistent.

Church and church clubs

Two thirds of the group attended church during primary school. During the secondary school years this figure dropped to 59 per cent. However, 77 per cent of those interviewed were involved in church activities and church clubs, mostly involved in planning and taking part in programmes, learning and reciting Bible scriptures and poetry, and studying the stories in the Bible.

These activities were generally seen as beneficial. When commenting on his Christianity and his involvement in church Marvin said:

> It gives you confidence. It gives you a standard and the reason not to do things. It gives you a better idea about consequences and rewards

and in the long run it gives you a more mature outlook on things in general.

The theme of confidence was echoed by Aaron:

One would hope that a religious background would instil some kind of confidence, some kind of self-awareness and I suppose confidence is really the term to run with. Confidence seems to me to be one of the key factors and also something about self awareness.

Regular and active involvement in church activities characterised this group. They appeared to be willing to be involved.

Music tuition

Over half the successful group had music lessons, which appeared to be highly valued amongst the parents:

It's really because my dad is into it. By the time I was 10 I was very keen to play. I tried playing the recorder at school and then I wanted to play an instrument and my dad said 'What about piano?' because he liked piano. You know, whatever one did, you never had a choice... We did piano lessons. I got up to grade 4. (Charlene)

Glen noted the similarities between regular study and learning to play an instrument:

I had organ lessons. Yes, music was something that was dearly loved in our home. I was given the opportunity to learn an instrument and I had always been quite musical. I fancied myself as a bit of a percussionist, but organ came along, so I think it was good. I suppose there are similarities. In the same way you have to sort of study for exams you have to study for theory and stuff like that. I didn't actually take the exams, but I did study for the test because often they were on Sabbaths, on my day of worship. So I couldn't go through with them. But I was again sort of pushed and there was an outlet for that because I could play the organ. I could take that skill and play at church which was ideal. (Glen)

There was a dilemma for this respondent with music exams being on what was for him a religious day. Religious belief and music were both valued. So despite preparing for the examinations, Glen was unable to take them. The members of this group who had music tuition spoke positively about music tuition and taking graded examinations.

Other activities

Over half the group were involved in sports clubs after school, many participating in football and athletics. A number attended youth clubs and just under half of them made regular use of public libraries. Other activities that were engaged in were dance classes and study courses. Almost everyone was involved in some way in activities outside of school. These were all activities that required discipline and personal application to achieving goals, all characteristics that could be transferred to the academic learning environment.

Motivators and role models

Some of the people in the group talked about significant individuals who gave of their time and motivated them. Some were parents while others were other members of the family or community. The church emerged as a significant source of motivators enabling the relaying of experiential knowledge and the provision of positive support.

> I suppose it was other people in church. I had friends who were older and I think talking to them at church really allowed me to get a grip of what I really needed to do. I didn't understand the whole process. I spoke to a friend who told me that if you want to do A-levels you've got to get these GCSEs. I knew that much. In my limited understanding I thought I should just take the subjects where I know I can sort of excel. (Glen)

Another schoolboy, Simon, was motivated by the encouragement given to him by others

> Talking to different people and them saying basically, 'You've gone past the halfway mark, just finish it. You're good enough to do it.' Just encouragement really. (Simon).

The High Fliers were the only group that shared experiences of having role models and motivators, from within the community. Forty six per cent spoke about people who were role models for them, ranging from the famous to family friends. The success of Ben Carson, a world famous Black surgeon who came from a poor background, was motivating for Fiona:

> ...I read the book about Ben Carson and that really inspired me and I really wanted to be like him... It was before my GCSEs and I thought wow that really motivated me. (Fiona)

Others had role models who were closer to home. For four of the group they were friends of the family or their own friends:

> Yeah, it has to be my best friend, his mum. She is a head of a police department ...I mean she's done really well. She couldn't afford to go to Uni or anything like that. But like she's just finished doing her Masters degree and everything. So it would be his Mum. I still see her now and she is constantly reminding me to 'make sure you do well in your A levels' and she is probably my biggest role model. (Joshua)

> And I've been inspired by the sorts of friends, close friends, church friends, again. I think again I've seen and observed the things that they do and I can say yes, it's good. I have been surrounded by a lot of positive people and I think that it just helped. Not necessarily just any individual or individuals but also in terms of the group effort in helping me. (Glen)

> ... People in the church would give me encouragement. They would give me a lot of examples about things that they had accomplished and how they did it. So I was really inspired by them. (Marvin)

Thus role models and the advice they offered were an influential part of the experiences of the High Fliers.

School

Overall, the High Fliers described feeling positive about school. While most attended comprehensive schools and described these as having a positive ethos that encouraged excellence and achievement, a few attended grant maintained, grammar, private or church schools.

School ethos

When reflecting on their school years, the High Fliers talked about the impressions they had of school, its ethos and the messages explicitly and implicitly transmitted within school. They commented on the academic and behavioural standards of the school and whether it was viewed as a 'good' school.

> Oh there was definitely an atmosphere of working hard and doing your best. It was quite academic and people were expected to pass all of their exams. That was the general tone of things. (Neville)

> ... They were very keen on you being the best person you can be. Very keen on people having goals, having dreams, having aims, knowing what they want to do from a very early age and trying their best to pursue that and to be that. And I always felt that even though they encouraged us to strive for excellence, I think there was more of an emphasis on being the best that you can be. (Trent)

The members of this group reported receiving positive messages, encouragement to work hard, exhortations to do their best and strive for standards of excellence in their work. They described their school and its reputation as 'good' in relation to academic standards, positive attitudes, and having a strong disciplinary code.

Despite the messages of encouragement and achievement transmitted in school and the disciplined, achievement oriented ethos and atmosphere, some underlying negative issues were revealed by some of the comments.

> Yes I remember them [school] having this merit system ... if you did well on such and such a thing you would get a merit mark. All the merit marks were added together and I'm not entirely sure what you actually received. But a merit mark was like a gold nugget, it was something to be desired... I don't know, it seemed to capture the hearts of all the pupils. And I remember my first merit mark was not for anything academic. Actually, it seems silly but it was for walking across the stage with a book on my head. I think I proved the theory or something [laughs] for it was like to give a Black student a merit

mark for something not academic... but I think they gave them out willy-nilly. (Glen)

Glen laughed when he told this story, indicating that he felt strongly that it was so ridiculous that it was laughable. But he went on to relate other occasions where he was awarded a merit mark. Those that stood out in his mind were for non-academic acts like being polite at the dentist, noticed by the headteacher; however, he received merits for academic work too, but could not recall anything specific. Glen believed that as a Black pupil he was expected to value merit marks for non-academic acts rather than for academic ones.

One young woman who attended a highly successful grammar school felt a sense of inadequacy or of being just average, and also had a sense of being treated differently.

I mean 6 O-levels [former secondary school qualification] were okay, but there were other children who had about 10 or 11 O-levels. And it made me feel really stupid compared with them. And then you talk to these other people in the shop and they are like, 'Well I didn't get any O-levels' or 'I only got one CSE [former lower status secondary school qualification] and I only got this'. Then you think, well maybe, we're not quite as bad but at school because it had such a high reputation and most people did do very well they treated you slightly differently, if you weren't like career orientated. (Jolene)

Although, the High Fliers generally attended schools with a positive ethos conveying encouragement and motivation, some of them had sensed that the messages of focusing, aiming high and doing their best were aimed at other pupils but not at them.

Teachers and teaching

The High Fliers had helpful teachers overall, who were positive and encouraging, but this was qualified in many cases by accounts of one or two teachers who were unhelpful or with whom they had a negative experience

A couple of them were good, a couple of them were very encouraging. But there were a few, obviously, of the old school – they didn't really want to encourage me at all. ... Some of them didn't want me to take my A-levels [advance level examinations used to gain access to university] they wanted me to leave school at 16 and do nursery nursing or anything else because they didn't think I would be able to do my A-levels. But I proved them wrong. And I stayed there for sixth form. (Jolene)

All the High Fliers described teachers who spent time with them and with whom they could identify.

I think I was treated fairly and then I think in my later years there was a tutor that I had and she did take time out to actually help me. I think she was my English teacher, she even wanted to come round to help me do some work. (Simon)

The High Fliers experienced affirmation and positive support from some of their teachers but most (77%) acknowledged individual teachers who were less than supportive.

Attitude towards school

Fifty five percent of the High Fliers said that they had positive attitudes towards their secondary school experiences. Twenty one percent described them as being mixed or negative. The number of those in the group who described their secondary school experiences positively was high in comparison with the other four groups.

Unpleasant experiences at school

Twenty three per cent of the High Fliers recalled unpleasant experiences at school. Charlene loved English but her English teacher did not consider her good enough to do the Advanced level (A-level) English course.

... And of course for A-levels there was very little choice in what I wanted to do so English was definitely going to be one of them because I enjoyed that. And I really had no idea what the others [subjects] would be but they almost put me off taking it because she didn't think I was that good at English, which might be a teacher thing really. But they obviously had spotted that I enjoyed it especially. In those days enjoyment was not enough and I wasn't a bad student by any means, but they were like 'No I don't think you should do A-level English.' And I felt that was a bit unfair really. (Charlene)

I just remembered, I had one incident with the physics teacher at the end of year nine going on to do my GCSEs you had to do an exam to see whether you would be in a high group or low group. I passed to go to the higher group, but the teacher didn't feel I was confident enough to be in a high group and he put me in the low group. But I should have been in a high group because of my results. My dad went to see the teacher and he had to sort it out and put me back in the group I was supposed to be in. He wasn't too pleased about that. (Fiona)

So the teachers' judgements about a pupil's abilities were sometimes inaccurate. This raises questions about teacher assessment and the influence teachers have over a pupil's future. But others in the group did not recall any negative experiences.

Not personally, no. I am not sure whether it was because I hung around the wrong people that the teachers didn't even need to hassle me or I wasn't kind of a naughty child. But at the same time I didn't get in the way of the teachers enough for them to have to be telling me off. So I'm not sure whether that is my own doing which prevented them from getting at me. (Aaron)

If there were problems there I wasn't necessarily caught up in them. I suppose it was still a case of if there were [problems] you were still going to succeed at school and even if there was racism you were going to succeed. (Glen)

Thus does Glen explain his motivation for avoiding trouble at school. His parents' belief that problems should not prevent you from studying and doing well, meant that whatever the obstacles, the route to success must be followed. Most of the group were able to avoid negative incidents and maintained positive feelings about school. Charlene speaks for many of the group:

> I loved the whole experience of being at school getting new know-ledge. I enjoyed the friendships and then the social side of it. The only thing I regret was the fact that they never made reference to any Black issues at all. It was definitely not on the curriculum and it was interesting that no matter how much history we did there was no mention of Black people doing anything. (Charlene)

Not all experiences were positive but this group tended to see any negative incidents as unusual so they did not affect their overall feelings about their school experience. Some of them had consciously tried to avoid trouble at school so as to minimise any potential problems. Taken as a whole, the High Fliers were positive about their schooling and felt they were unaffected by negative experiences.

Exclusion and truancy

Only two of the High Fliers experienced fixed term exclusions in primary school. There were none in secondary school nor any permanent exclusions. However, when informal exclusion was explored it turned out that 14 per cent had been sent home from school or made to work away from class for more than a day. Only two of the High Fliers admitted to truanting, one on their own in primary school and one in both sectors. Not all truanted for whole days, though they regularly missed certain lessons. Some considered their exclusions to have been unfair although Trent regarded his as justified:

> It was actually while we were fighting that we knocked over a teacher. This teacher started coming between us while we were fighting. And we knocked the teacher over so I think that was fair and both of us were suspended. It was for three days. I think we had a fight on Tuesday and they said, 'don't come back to school for the rest of the week'. (Trent)

Although Trent accepted his responsibility for knocking over the teacher he was surprised and pleased at his mother's reaction to what happened:

...She stood up for me actually, because she knew I wasn't that type of person I do not, I mean, if I'm in a fight then it would be because people are picking on me or I'm defending myself. But that really pleased me actually about her attitude because I remember her saying to the headmaster, 'I know my son'. (Trent)

Despite the failure of the school to consider what caused the fight, Trent was pleased that his mother raised the matter with the head teacher. It was also clear that both boys received equal punishment.

Qualifications

In addition to the 5 GCSE A*-C grades attained, 90 per cent of the High Fliers went on to achieve other qualifications. Figure 3.1 shows the highest qualifications they achieved.

More than half (52%) of the High Fliers achieved at least a BA/BSc qualification and 17 per cent achieved MA degrees or other postgraduate qualifications. Having achieved five GCSEs at the

Figure 3.1: Highest qualification achieved by the High Fliers

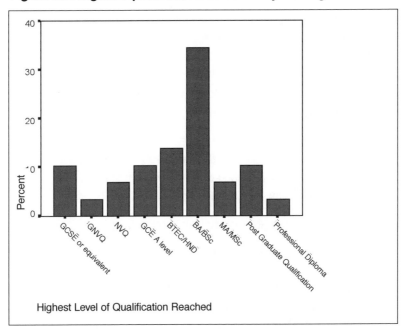

end of secondary school does not necessarily mean pursuit of post graduate qualifications or, indeed, a first degree but there was a trend in this direction.

Perceived Success Factors

At interview the participants were asked what they felt contributed to their academic achievement at school. They named parents and home environment, school influences, friends, role models, religious belief and individual characteristics. Individuals also attributed their success to a combination of factors. Their perceived reasons for their success are described here.

Home

Most (62%) of the High Fliers attributed their success to their parents. They described their parents pushing and encouraging them.

> I have to say my parents kind of pushed me a lot. My teachers, yes they made me do it too. Really, I don't know. I knew I had to do it because I was expected to go to school and university too. (Barbara).

> I would say it was mum and dad more and other relatives that pushed me rather than the school. (Jolene)

Individual

Forty six per cent mentioned individual success factors. Some respondents were very clear about how they had achieved:

> I think it's really more that I knew there were certain subjects I was weak on I knew that there were certain subjects I was strong on and that I just liked. So I just worked with the ones that I was the strongest on and the ones that I needed. (Glen)

They also acknowledged ability as contributing to success:

> But it depends. I could study anywhere and that was a thing that they [parents] couldn't understand. I could study anywhere. Like now, sometimes I'm doing something just before I go to the shop and I have a brainwave and pick up my book and I read and I will remember it. But I wouldn't actually sit down for a long time. (Barbara).

> I'm not extremely intelligent like Einstein, but I'm not dumb. So I think I've got that natural ability to be just above average. (Natasha)

Their understanding of themselves and their abilities helped the High Fliers to achieve.

Community

Four of the group identified friends who had influenced them and thus contributed to their achievements.

> In the last two years, there were four of us. And none of us were below average we were all like intelligent. So we did well. I suppose if one of us was below average then that might have pulled the others down. But we didn't feel different and our work didn't suffer. (Natasha)

> I have a White friend who I used to work for when I was about 15 and we've remained good friends up until this day. And he encouraged me also of the value of going to university and he was actually a very important influence on my life...and so he was such an important part of my life. (Trent)

Only the High Fliers talked about having friends who played a part in their achievement.

School

School was referred to in conjunction with other factors; 46 per cent of the High Fliers saw school as contributing to their success and especially certain teachers:

> For mathematics, it would be a teacher and I had him from year 8 to year 10. But he was one of the best teachers I have ever had and the way that he taught, everybody did the sums. He predicted that I would get A* for Mathematics...We'd go back to him for extra lessons. But apart from that I don't really think anybody influenced me that much. (Natasha)

> And also in the later years of secondary school they bought like this Afro-Caribbean guy I think they've got this sort of system where they send them in some of the schools now. So he used to come into some of our classes sit down with the African Caribbean children and

> he used to come in my English class. Yeah, he used to put a bit of pressure on and he used to say you need to get this done here and this done in the other. (Simon)

This quote supports the use of Black mentors in schools. Simon clearly remembers this man and attributes his own success to the encouragement the mentor gave Black pupils to get their work done.

Trent spoke about his predominately Black church school:

> As for going to university I think that school was a key factor. They always encouraged their students to go on to university. (Trent)

Although less than half of the High Fliers attributed their academic success to school factors, these respondents indicate that school can be influential. The various ecosystems that the High Fliers interacted with – school, home, and community – provided broadly positive experiences. The negative experiences they mentioned all took place at school, although these were not dwelt upon or imbued with strong feelings of having been subjected to injustice or racism.

4

Eagles who Soar:
The Retakers

The Retakers achieved at least 5 GCSE A*-C grades (or equivalent) after they left school. All were over 31 years old. This group made up 12 per cent (10) of the whole sample, and 60 per cent of the group were women and 40 per cent male. It had the highest percentage of people (80%) of people employed in professional occupations and only one was a full time student.

Home
Education valued by parents

The Retakers were brought up primarily in homes where parents valued education. The Retakers and High Fliers were the two groups which most consistently reported that their parents had positive attitudes to their education. Parents passed on these messages about the importance of education to their children:

> There was no compromise. You had to get an education. I mean my dad would verbally say 'You've got to go to school and study...' And I suppose it was also the case that in Jamaica, if you want to have good education you had to pay for it, but come to this country you didn't have to pay for it. It was free and so you needed to take advantage of it and make the most of what you've got. (Anita)

> I think part of their main desire was for me to do better than what they had accomplished. Their desire was for us to excel and they made it plain that they never had the opportunities and advantages that we had. (Rohan)

The message is clear that education was an opportunity to be seized. The parents' desire for their children to have an education and to excel was a message that was absorbed and internalised.

Most of the parents positively encouraged their children:

> They always wanted, well, initially encouraged me to do well. I initially wanted to become a doctor, and they encouraged me to go in that direction. Sometimes it was a bit too heavy for me but they were always very willing to push you in the right direction. (Dominic)

> From quite an early age, I remember when we were at junior school; they always used to encourage us to go to the library quite a bit. Obviously when we went to the library what books we took out, that was another story. They used to always be quite up on your reading, the spelling, and the English and of course we had to read in church. (Josie)

The parents' specific acts of encouragement and support were sufficient for these respondents to absorb the message that they were expected to do well. However, there was generally little evidence of parents actively giving them practical assistance through the provision of educational resources and close supervision or monitoring of their academic activity.

Homework and routines

Few of these parents provided practical assistance with homework or educational resources and the group showed less consistent patterns of homework completion than the High Fliers. Most reported completing homework but not as part of their evening routine.

> Yes, I can't remember the teachers telling me off, or getting into trouble, for not doing my homework. It might be the night before or on the bus going to school, but I did get it done. (Anita)

Anita talked about her teachers' involvement but not her parents. Only 30 per cent of this group reported having help with homework during primary school and only 40 per cent during secondary school. Furthermore only 10 per cent reported this help as coming from their parents, although some parents did ensure that homework was completed.

> I think they did their best in that they went to parents' evening and made sure you did your homework but that was it. But you can survive on doing the minimum. I didn't find the work particularly hard, so I could leave it to the last minute, play and do whatever you had to do and 'Have you done your homework?' 'Yes, I've done it. Look I've finished it.' Rather than getting an A, I'd get a probably get a C. (Josie)

> Unless I had any social activities, which was not as often as I would have liked. But if I had any social activities and I had to go then I would be allowed to do them as well. But I couldn't go to bed at night without doing my homework. (Dominic)

These examples show little evidence of a set routine concerning homework. Although homework was completed it was not always done to the highest standards. Given that fewer of these parents were educated beyond secondary schooling and fewer were employed in professional occupations than the High Fliers it may not be surprising that few of these parents provided practical assistance with homework. The Retakers were less consistent in completing homework than the High Fliers, neither was homework part of a regular routine at home. Unlike many parents in the High Fliers group, only 20 per cent of the Retakers reported that their parents distrusted the education system.

Individual

Certain personal characteristics were deemed to have contributed to academic success, notably personal motivation and religious belief .

Motivation

Motivation was described in terms of having an awareness of one's capabilities and a desire to achieve.

> I knew what I was capable of doing and I realised that even when I was hanging with a lot of my peers, who were very much more into the sports and music rather than the academic side, I was quite influenced by them. But when I left school obviously realising what I had actually achieved I thought to myself that I could go on and do so much better. So really the second time round I actually motivated myself. (Dominic)

> I think I was highly self motivated yes I was highly self motivated. I wanted to do well and excel and let them feel proud of me, but that wasn't the sole motivating aspect. I think because I wanted to do well I wanted to succeed it was to prove that I was capable of doing well. (Rohan)

Rohan went on to describe his motivation as coming from two additional sources: being keen to make his parents proud of him, and wanting to prove his abilities. And he wanted to prove people wrong:

> If people had a certain expectation of me which I think wasn't worthy of what I could do, my challenge was to prove them wrong and I think that's always stuck with me. So I do remember there were one or two teachers who gave me the impression that perhaps I wasn't capable of doing very well, so that would give me a challenge to prove them wrong, to do well. That's where my self motivation came from. (Rohan)

Thus Rohan had several motivational influences to achieve his goals. The Retakers did not demonstrate a clear pattern of motivation. Two other respondents described themselves as being highly self motivated but were thrown off track by peers. Some said that they really had no clear idea of what motivated them.

> I have no idea. It could be ambition. It could be that my self esteem is quite high and I value myself and know that I have not reached my full potential and I think probably that maybe I owe it to myself to say yes you are capable even though you were probably never really made to feel that. (Josie)

Josie hints that being made to feel that she was not capable was something she had to overcome and this contributed to her taking longer than she expected to achieve her goals. Norman said he was not interested in academic success but in getting a trade:

> Looking back on school I think that I did not look beyond doing a trade. When I went to the careers advisors they would always talk about this kind of thing. (Norman)

Norman's comments suggest that careers advice received inhibited his aspirations, yet he pursued academic qualifications and achieved them after completing school.

Religious belief

Forty percent of the Retakers referred to religious belief. Norman attributed his eventual achievement to the philosophy of the church:

> I would probably think that it was the philosophy of the church the philosophy of using to the fullest what God has given to you. Being the best you can because God expects no less. (Norman)

Anita talked about putting God's will above her own wishes:

> I always ask the Lord what he wants. I suppose that sounds a bit strange. And certainly now I know what I want to do in education and what I want to achieve. If it's not what he wants me to do, then I would have to work within his will.

Religious belief was an important factor in the lives of some of the High Fliers and Retakers.

Individual problems and difficulties

As with the High Fliers, 40 per cent of the Retakers described having problems such as lack of motivation and guidance.

> I studied hard but I was not successful and that's probably why I didn't pass all the exams that I took. I don't know why that might have been. I suppose I was still using my own tactics, my own methods of studying and I didn't get any guidance. (Anita)

I don't think I studied. I think that a few of my teachers saw the ability but I was more interested in cricket and just sports generally. Not that I was really into anything in particular, but I don't think that I was really that focused to say I was really going to knuckle down and study. So I would actually put it down to that more than lack of encouragement. I wasn't focused; I wasn't self motivated. (Norman)

Lack of focus and poor study skills contributed to the failure of the Retakers to achieve success in exams at the end of secondary school.

Community

This group reported similar levels of involvement in community activities to the High Fliers but their experiences were less consistent and less positive. They had the highest number of role models from the community and the highest levels of attendance at church, youth clubs and libraries.

Church and church clubs

Seventy per cent regularly attended church services during primary school and 90 per cent during secondary school.

I had to be there ... I helped out in some of the Holiday Bible schools that we had sometimes. I helped out as a teacher there as well. (Dominic)

Their participation in the work of their churches extended to teaching, helping out and working in the community. There were however, aspects of church life they did not enjoy.

I think because of the nature of their [parents'] work in the church there was a lot of community work. There was always the youth club and the Sunday school and going around witnessing to people. We hated it. We used to have to stand up in the middle of town doing open air services. (Josie)

However, they were also emphatic that church enabled the development of skills seen only in those involved with church activities:

The Black church was a clear distinction between me and them and the discipline. Even now to be honest, I look at Black children that haven't been through that and there is a difference in the way they behave and it really makes a difference between your discipline and their discipline. The whole thing about respect for people and listening. You had to sit there from a small age ...we went through all levels of the church. We saw behind the scenes as well. It wasn't just attending and going home. We were putting out the chairs and putting the chairs away. And I used to watch my parents making the bread for Holy Communion. I used to watch them pouring out the wine... But if it wasn't for that church background I don't know what or where my influence would have been. I think it would have been Black but it would have been more if they were say party goers it would have been that sort of environment. But I am grateful it was that sort of healthy environment. (Josie)

Josie emphasises the influence of parents as role models. Having parents who were active in the church on whom to model behaviour was perceived as preferable to parents being involved in other aspects of community:

I think though that I feel that the Black church has always been very significant to the success and performance of Black children. In many senses, the church has been very central to community life. I am very concerned that the church is becoming less and less significant in the lives of my generation. I am not sure that this is going to be a good thing for our Black children academically. I do believe that those who understand and believe that God wants the best from us and instil that in their children tend to get much better results academically, educationally and so forth. (Norman)

Norman expressed concern about the decline of the Black church in the lives of the Black community, fearing that this could be detrimental to the academic development of Black children. These respondents felt that church involvement was a significant factor in their lives and helped develop characteristics that were beneficial to academic pursuits such as working towards the completion of tasks in clubs, teaching younger children and being involved with, participating, planning and running church programmes.

Music tuition

Half the group had music tuition during primary school but in secondary school this figure dropped to 30 per cent.

> I used to do music, the piano. Outside of school I had piano lessons... It was just me who liked music and because I used to do it at school, I came home and said that I wanted to learn to play the piano. Well, that was a big struggle in the home so I didn't keep it up for long. Although I can do a little on the piano, it was something that I really wanted to do but I wasn't really encouraged. It was too much money and so on. (Anita)

Dominic also received instrumental lessons and also sang and performed:

> ...A lot of weekends were spent where I used to do a lot of singing with some of the music schools we had in the area. I used to be doing work with different musical companies... And that was actually it. It was just sports and music really...I had vocal tuition and I did piano lessons when I was a lot younger. (Dominic)

None of the group mentioned taking music examinations.

Other activities

Less than half the group were involved in sports activities, only one made regular visits to the museum but use of local libraries was highest of all groups, at 60 per cent. All were involved in activities within the community that provided a focus outside of school.

Motivators and role models

As with the High Fliers, almost all the group cited role models:

> There were several males in church who had achieved well and had gone on to university etc. They were quite motivating for me because my thing was if somebody else could get to get there then I could do

so as well. Realistically, I felt that looking to these Black male role models helped me to get to where I wanted to get more. (Dominic)

I think I look back and probably one individual, no, more than one, but a young man who came from Guyana called CB. He was an outstanding chap around our kind of age about a year or so older, possibly. But he was just so focused, he came to do what he came to do and he was doing so well and I think that motivated me. (Norman)

There is a clear pattern in the highest achieving groups for role models to influence lives and remain a reference to point for advice and encouragement.

School

Most of the Retakers were positive about their school experiences, although some said their schools did not have a positive ethos. There were few accounts of schools giving encouraging, motivating or supportive messages. Nearly all the group had attended comprehensive schools but one had attended an independent church school.

School ethos

Fewer group members than the High Fliers described their schools as 'good': schools which transmitted positive messages and had high academic expectations. Some did attend such schools but most did not. They went to schools where the reputation was not perceived as good and there was no clear ethos of achievement or of encouragement to pupils to work hard and do their best.

I went to a comprehensive not known for its great reputation. I don't think the school was great in terms of turning out, in the sense that it was not known for its passes and so forth. It was an average school. There were people who did well, but I think the majority were below average, probably. (Norman)

No I don't think I picked up any philosophy of the school. I didn't get a clear message about studying from school, I got it from home. (Anita)

...I think the ethos of school was more to do with conduct and behaviour, discipline and respect for teachers and maintaining the image of the school. Not so much on doing your best, striving and things like that. (Rohan)

Teachers

Contrary to the High Fliers, the Retakers all reported feeling unsupported by their teachers and being subject to negative stereotyping. Although 40 per cent acknowledged encountering some good teachers, this did not characterise their view of their teachers.

The teachers seemed to be really nice, you know. Some of them, you could tell who was racist; I think that you get to know that and you can sort of live with that... What they did encourage you in, because I remember I was good at sports, to do the sports and I remember the PE teacher would encourage me in sports. But nobody stands out that helped me. (Anita)

Anita reports receiving encouragement in sporting activities but she observes that her teachers did not help or encourage her in other areas. Two respondents who described similar experiences found problems when they wanted to engage in class discussions and ask questions:

But I don't feel that a lot of the teachers actually spent time encouraging, well me personally, in the fields that I had wanted to do. I felt they didn't know how to deal with someone like myself; I am very strong-minded and always wanted to answer questions. Subjects in which I excelled were things like religious studies and science and English, those primarily because you weren't just being fed information. But you weren't encouraged to participate in discussion, in debate. In the other classes when you asked questions it was like, well it's not your place to ask those kinds of questions so you felt marginalised. (Dominic)

I think it was the teachers' attitude towards me, say for example, in maths. I always remember I wasn't particularly hot on maths, anyway. But I remember, if I didn't understand something I would always ask

> 'Well why are we doing this', or ask a question and I was always told that your problem is that you question too much, you ask too many questions. (Josie)

While identifying a few teachers as exceptions, the group all reported a lack of support from their teachers.

Attitude to school

Most of the Retakers described themselves as having positive attitudes towards their secondary school experiences rather than negative feelings. However, in the interviews they described negative experiences in some detail.

Negative experiences

Most of the group reported having negative experiences with teachers and other pupils. They spoke about being placed in inappropriate subject sets, being the target of racist name calling, and fear of attack as well as involvement in fights. Dominic described the de-motivating experience of being placed in what he felt was the wrong Maths set:

> For example, I had left primary school in the top maths stream and came to secondary school and was thrust into doing a maths test straight away and somehow ended up in group 4 of 6 which is very de-motivating. But it was corrected by the second year, when I obviously raised a protest against it and got my parents involved and I was moved up to the second class. By the end of my second year I was in the second class and then stayed there basically until the end of school. I felt that I could have gone into the first class but I don't think it was encouraged. (Dominic)

This was not the only negative experience Dominic mentioned. He recalled occasions where he was called names:

> There were obviously, being in the minority, occasions when set euphemisms were used – 'brown boy, Black boy' etc., etc., that was mainly from students. (Dominic)

Other respondents had been involved in fights at school:

> I used to fight and when I got into the secondary school you know your reputation goes before you. So I realised that everybody wanted to fight me, that was boys as well. And so I did start to fight back. (Anita)

While reflecting on this, Anita made a link between the fighting and the long-term illness and ultimately the death of her mother during these years.

> My mum was sick for a long while and died when I was 11. But then to me I didn't associate it [fighting] with that. But you know as an adult you look back and if the child was to display that kind of behaviour that mother was sick at home you'd associate it all with that. But I didn't feel that at the time. I was not really a bully but if someone troubled me then I would fight back. I was rarely the one to start fighting. But people would come to fight you because they knew you would fight back. (Anita)

> Yes, there were a few [problems]. I noticed that some of the White girls would make trouble or call you names or whatever and when push came to shove and you had a fight they always came off worse. (Josie)

But because she was able to defend herself in the fights, Josie encountered further problems.

> I remember we had a fight and I pulled this girl's hair out and I left it, I think I just threw it ...and I got called in by the teacher and she had all this like stuff in her hand and she asked 'What's this? What is this?' ... She said it is Rebecca whatever her name's hair and she said, 'How dare you pull her hair out.' And I said 'Well we had a fight and that's what happened', and she said 'If two 9 year olds have a fight they should end up in the same state and not with one in her state and one in your state.' I don't remember what the fight was about but I know I wasn't the trouble maker because with my upbringing I was very very aware of not to start trouble. (Josie)

Rohan feared racist attacks:

> The area where I went to school was a predominately White area and during my time at school we had the year of the Mods, the skinheads.

We had a lot of that inside the school, in fact it was an experience every day to leave the school. They used to hang around the gates of the school. Some of them were students of the school in the upper years. So that was always an experience. We did experience a high degree of racism when it came to other students and because we were in a minority – it wasn't just Black pupils but there were also a lot of Asians, as well. They seemed to be the main target of racist attacks that really took place inside the school in the playground and outside the school gates... And also there were times when even though I wasn't the subject of racism or racist attacks there was always that thought that you could be next. That was always a dramatic experience... So there was always that fear, I mean I wasn't attacked in any way or physically harmed. You know you have comments that were made but you just dealt with those but there was always that concern about what will tomorrow bring. (Rohan)

The Retakers clearly recalled such events and described them without hesitation. Their experiences suggested a sense of not feeling accepted and feeling alienated from the school community.

Going back to the Junior school it was quite a White school. I remember not quite fitting in because my home background was very stable but it was also very different to all my White colleagues'. My parents were ministers and so obviously my weekends were very different to their weekends. They would go to see Nana while we were going to Sunday school, evening service and probably a convention on the Saturday. In the summer holidays there were a lot of conventions in the week. There were a lot of Bible study, prayer meetings, Youth clubs etc. I do actually remember that we used to have to write stories about what you did at the weekend and of course I would make it up 'I went to Alton Towers.' Only I [actually] went to Birmingham to Pastor So and So's church... or I went to London but I didn't write about that because I knew it was different. I didn't want to be different so I used to make it up. (Josie)

Clearly, Josie was aware that her lifestyle differed from those of her schoolmates. The fact that she felt she had to make up stories about her weekend activities indicates her sense of insecurity and a feeling that her lifestyle would not be accepted by her peers or would make her appear different.

Unpleasant school experiences were not always the fault of the teaching staff – many had to do with other children. But no one found the teachers supportive or understanding. As the interviewees reflected on their experiences it was clear that the negative experiences they had at school were important events which stood out in their minds and which some of them spoke about with strong emotion.

Exclusion and truancy

Twenty percent of the Retakers were excluded for a fixed term while in secondary school. None had been made to work away from their class and only one had experienced informal exclusion by being sent home during primary school. Ten per cent admitted truanting from school and 20 per cent skipped classes while at school. Yet not all of them described being excluded for a fixed period of time for fighting with a strong sense of injustice, as we heard from other groups. Anita talked about having a reputation for fighting, and being excluded for getting into a fight:

> ...I got into trouble once. I was suspended once – that never happened again... I was suspended from school for a couple of days... I would just have been at home. I think I didn't want to leave that school. I was more worried about my dad when the letter got to him. I was more scared about that. I think it was a two-day suspension and then come back, as opposed to your parents having to come into school. My dad was really angry but at the same time talking to me. I always wanted to be at school so there was no problem me going back. (Anita)

Anita talked about her exclusion as something that simply happened, giving the impression that it was justified and that it had no special significance. This was not the case with Dominic. He did not take his exclusion experience lightly and recalled it with a strong sense of injustice.

I was suspended from school. I was suspended in the third year at school for reacting to the behaviour of a dinner lady. It was a temporary exclusion, it was a suspension and the statement was that because of my previous behaviour and because of the commendations from other teachers who obviously felt ... that this was out of character for me, it was noted as a cooling down period for me, but it was still placed on my record. The dinner lady manhandled me in this situation which was totally not my fault and I reacted by physically pushing her off me. And as a result they said they had no choice but to suspend me because if not what message will this give out to other students. (Dominic)

When asked about how he felt, Dominic replied:

Embarrassed and very bitter as nothing was really done to the woman who had actually caused the incident in the first place. He described his feelings as he looked back on the incident: To a certain extent I still feel bitter but not to the extent that it is a grudge that's been held onto. But certainly if it's one rule for one, it definitely should be the same rule for another.

Dominic's sense of injustice was strong and has remained so even today. Although recognising that this behaviour was out of character for their son, his parents were unhappy and embarrassed about the situation and the way it had been dealt with. It is debatable whether Dominic, whose previous behaviour was considered to be such that teachers made commendations about him, should have had the exclusion recorded or even should have been excluded.

Qualifications

Of the ten members of the Retakers group one had a Doctorate, three had Bachelor degrees. The majority of the group went on to pursue academic qualifications ranging from A-levels to a Doctorate. (See figure 4.1 on page 62)

A consideration of how long it took this group to achieve five GCSE exam passes after secondary schooling shows that half of the group took one additional year. One took two years and two

Figure 4.1: Highest Qualifications Attained by the Retakers

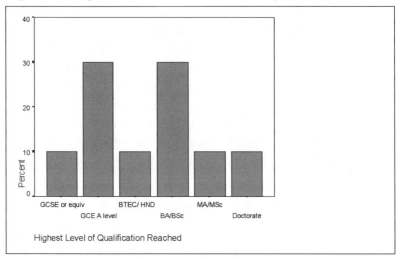

took three years to achieve 5 GCSE passes at grades A*-C. Most of the group retook their exams in Sixth Form or Further Education (FE) College.

Reasons for failing exams

The Retakers were asked to consider why they had not passed at lease 5 GCSEs at A*-C grades at secondary school. About one third attributed it to factors within their homes and one indicated lack of support from his parents. Others said that it was down to themselves. But 50 per cent of the group attributed their failure to lack of support and encouragement at school.

Perceived success factors

Three respondents answered the question regarding success and who they attributed it to but only one referred to their parents' influence:

> I think on the whole it's your parents, but then at school especially in the secondary school I had two friends and we all did the same..., but yes, the home and friends really. (Anita)

Self motivation and religious belief were cited by 60 per cent of the group as the reasons for succeeding academically after school. They did not report any community or school factors in their success.

The Retakers attributed their failure in school exams to school and their own lack of motivation. One of them reported having special educational needs. There was no overall pattern of positive experiences in any of the ecosystems they encountered: home, school or community. However their experiences were closer to those described by the High Fliers than to those of the Underachievers.

5

Eagles who Soar:
The Perseverers

The Perseverers were distinctive: all had bachelor degrees but they did not satisfy the criteria for membership of the other two achievement groups. In other words they did not have at least 5 GCSEs A*-C grades or equivalent. The Perseverers were all over 26 years old and most were over 31. They made up 18 per cent (14) of the whole sample of whom six were interviewed. The high proportion (64%) of men in the Perseverers group was statistically significant – it was not due to chance. Half the Perseverers were employed in professional occupations and it had the highest percentage of full time students of all the groups.

Home
Education valued by parents

This group's experiences were similar in some ways to the High Fliers' but in other ways parallelled the Underachievers'. As with the High Fliers their parents had very positive attitudes to education. This was true of slightly more of the mothers (79%) than fathers (64%). Almost one third (29%) of fathers were reported to have neutral attitudes to education, whereas the mothers' attitudes were comparable to those of the parents of the highest achieving groups, High Fliers and Retakers.

Half of those interviewed recalled hearing about the importance of education from their parents. But other factors may have reduced the impact of the verbal positive messages. Robert, who got into difficulties at school and had a number of fixed term exclusions, described the messages he received about education:

> Well that was one of the reasons why they used to discipline me, because they said that education is so important and vital because in their country you could never get it. You could never really get what we get here in this country. So they used to say. 'Study! Be something, be ambitious. If I were in your position and in your situation I wouldn't take everything for granted. Just utilise it because you're very fortunate we have not got what you've got.' So you know, basically they pushed me, impressed me to do good and be ambitious. (Robert)

Robert was physically punished at home, particularly when he was excluded from school. So although he was receiving positive messages to achieve they were tempered with physical discipline. This did not seem to further his parents' aims, since his behaviour at school did not improve.

Dionne also recalls her parent's encouraging messages:

> Yes, I grew up with both my mother and father wanting or expressing the need for us to excel in school; and hearing each day that as black young people and as a woman you have to do two or three times better than a White person in my situation in order to excel or to get on in life. And so I had that before me all the time. And with me they had higher expectations anyway. I don't know whether it's because I was a girl and the eldest. (Dionne)

For Dionne the message was consistent. However, she also had the responsibility of caring for her younger siblings and this made it difficult for her to achieve her potential:

> I was responsible for my younger siblings, more so in the latter years of school, as the oldest of four and the only girl. My mother worked evenings, she worked very long hours and my father was out as well. So being the older person I was responsible for the babies, the chil-

dren. So that was a major disruption for me to look after the children during those years.

Marcus also recalled his parents' encouragement:

> They would say 'Come you've got homework to do.' There was no tricking. But with my homework I don't think they would have understood what I was doing anyway.

Marcus recognised the difficulties his parents would have had trying to help him with his homework. Moreover, they worked long hours to support a large family:

> My dad would start work at five in the morning and come home at midnight. And my mum had all of us to look after. There were eight of us and there was no way she would have been able to sit down to go through books.

The interviewees were fully aware of their parents' high regard for education and remembered what they had said. But other circumstances affected the impact of these positive messages.

Participants in every group recalled their parents' positive messages, but for some groups, particularly the Underchievers and the Perseverers, these messages were not supported by practical help and encouragement.

Parents providing practical help

Only two in this group reported receiving practical support. Samuel was supported through the provision of resources:

> I went through all the tests that I should have gone through to pass the 11 plus exam. I had all the books at home for this and went through all of them. I could have got into the grammar school easily but every single evening I played football, every single evening. My parents bought the books. I've forgotten what they were called but they accompany the intended tests. I kind of went through them. They didn't go through them with me, which I think was part of the problem so that didn't help my motivation so I wasn't supported in that sense. But they bought the books and expected me to go through them. Mum did a couple of spelling tests with me and that was about it.

> Then they would say go and look at the books and I would sneak out the house. (Samuel)

While his parents' practical support in providing resources and extra tuition was helpful Samuel, did not receive the individual attention that he needed, of working through the books with him and monitoring his activities. Accordingly, he chose to play football rather than study putting the resources provided to little use:

> My mum had a fairly strong influence and my dad to an extent. They kept on top of things but I had a way of disguising what I was really doing. So when they thought I was doing my homework I might have been doing something else. (Samuel)

Dionne described the support her mother gave her:

> I remember my mum fighting for me to go to the better school. She really did fight and push to get me in the better school. But I still wouldn't say it had really high standards but I was happy there.

Two of the Perseverers felt they lacked the support of their families:

> I hated my home life. I ran away from home. I mean my parents were very strict, particularly my dad. We hated it when he was around but mum was always out at work anyway and I used to have to look after my brothers myself and the others... (Chantelle)

When asked how her parents felt about her schooling, Chantelle replied,

> Well, they left it up to me. I don't think they really had the time or didn't have the know-how of how to help me they just left me... They didn't get involved in anything. They didn't encourage me in any way, such as going into this career or that career. The choice was left for me.

Home life for Chantelle was neither structured nor supportive of schoolwork. Moreover, taking responsibility for her siblings appeared to take precedence. Isaac too felt that the support he needed was not there, despite his mother's interest in his education:

> My mum was really into how I was doing. But that didn't really impress me; it didn't make me feel whole as a person. What matters is not how much you work or if people have more money, if they don't have love then they haven't got anything. (Isaac)

Isaac was concerned about the fact that his parents, and particularly his mother, were not loving towards him and made constant comparisons between him and his sister:

> I cannot speak for every Black family but for some of us who actually grew up in big families there is always this constant comparison. So I've never really expressed a desire to get an education. I wanted to be loved more than anything else and felt that was lacking. (Isaac)

Isaac lost interest in education because of his parents' negative attitude towards him and because they never praised his achievements:

> When I passed my electronics and I said 'I passed' and showed her my certificate, she said to me, 'Oh, well done, but who wants that though.' She didn't really care and my Dad had the same kind of blasé attitude.

Overall, the Perseverers were made aware by their parents about the importance of education and doing well but rarely followed up such encouraging words with positive action.

This may have been due to the parents' own education. 21 per cent had no formal education the highest percentage of all groups whose parents were without qualifications. More mothers had received secondary (29%) and further education (21%) than the fathers: 21 per cent and 14 per cent respectively.

Fifty per cent of mothers were employed in mainly Associate Professional and Technical occupations and most (64%) of the fathers worked in process, plant and machinery, primarily manual jobs. More of the Perservers' parents worked in these occupations than the parents of any other group, and this may have affected their children's education. More of the Under-achievers and Perseverers lacked the quality of support that they needed to ensure success at school than those in the High Fliers group.

Homework and routines

Ninety three percent of the Perseverers said that they received no help with homework in secondary school. Statistical analysis found these results highly significant, indicating a relationship between having no help with homework and underachieving at school. Only one reported to have had help with homework in secondary school. Thirty five percent had some help with homework but this was still low when compared to the other achievement groups.

Only one Perseverer completed homework when it was given and received help doing it. For a variety of reasons most of the others did not do their homework. When asked, Did you normally receive homework from school? Chantelle said, Yes but I struggled with my homework. I didn't get any help with it.

For others doing homework depended entirely on which teacher had set it.

> There was some homework but whether you did it depended upon what teacher you had because some teachers made sure you did your homework I remember we had a little woman for English.... We never messed about when we went to her classroom, you make sure you're on time and you do your homework. I made sure I did my homework for her. It didn't matter how late at night it was I did her homework. (Marcus)

Only three of the Perseverers described having a set routine at home, but for only two of them was homework part of it. Marcus took responsibility for setting his own routine without having help with his homework:

> What I used to do personally when I came in, I would take my school clothes off and put them down neatly and put my house clothes on and come down to dinner. And if I did have any homework to do I would do it after dinner. (Marcus)

The other respondent had a routine with homework as part of it:

> There were chores that I had to do. I had to do my homework and then there would be chores that had to be done and then there was dinner. (Robert)

Regularly completing homework as part of a home routine was not characteristic of the Perseverers group, although there were one or two exceptions.

Distrust of the education system

Like the Underachievers, the Perseverers' parents tended to be satisfied with the education their children were receiving:

> I think that they looked at it that the teachers were always right. It wasn't that they were always right but coming from a background in Jamaica and the teacher is the one who should be respected and if you are not achieving something then you are the problem. So their attitude towards school was good we all had to go there to learn. (Marcus)

Their trust in the school system contrasted with the views of parents of the High Fliers, and appeared to be a contributory factor in explaining the difference between the high and the low achievers.

Individual characteristics

Eighty three percent of the Perseverers spoke about self-motivation. Their accounts suggest that they were less motivated at school than later in their lives.

> I think that in the past, immaturity has proven that I can start things off very well but then I've found that for one reason or another I have not completed what I started, so I have changed. Because I know myself a lot better now and I know I have that type of character – I am very much more motivated. (Dionne)

> I loved my school but I didn't like all the people in it. Teachers were all right and if I had knuckled down I would probably have achieved more... I think what motivates me now is realising that we are all equal... (Isaac)

> I could have gotten into the grammar school but every single evening I played football. I seemed to lack a bit of motivation really in preparation for that. If I had put in the proper work at the time I would have done far better. My motivation has changed now. I'm motivated to be more successful because of my priorities. (Samuel)

All three admitted weak self-motivation while at school. Motivation developed over time, as they matured. Isaac's eventual realisation that everyone is equal as motivational needs to be seen alongside of his parents' constant unfavourable comparison of him with his sister. Despite their high levels of motivation as adults the Perseverers did not report having goals when they were at school. No individual or personal problems were reported.

Community

Community involvement varied from positive regular involvement in some activities similar to the High Fliers, to negative, inconsistent experiences and attendance rather like the Underachievers.

Church and church clubs

The Perseverers had considerable commitment to church and church club attendance throughout their school years. While at primary school, 43 per cent attended church and this increased to 57 per cent during secondary schooling. The Perseverers had the highest church club involvement during secondary schooling of all the achievement groups.

Most Perseverers attended church services and their involvement ranged from attendance to leading services and programmes.

> I was actively involved in church services by holding offices at church in the youth department and the Sabbath school department... I was involved as a teenager. The ethos of the church that I went to was that everybody had a part to play including younger members. And so with regards to planning services and actually executing them and

doing things in church, in the worship services, I was one of the leaders. We would have committees with lots of different people and there would be young people and older people and I was one of the younger people that got involved quite a lot. I was in a trainee leadership role. (Dionne)

I was in the choir during my teen years. I attended church regularly from about 6. But I also went to Sunday school up until the age of about 8. So I was going to Sunday school and I was going to church on Sabbath. That was for about two years and then I just continued going to church on Sabbath. (Samuel)

Dionne gave a detailed description of her involvement in church activities. Samuel indicated his involvement in the church choir. Others simply stated that they attended church but did not discuss being involved in any activities:

I went to church services right the way through primary and secondary school. Yes but in primary school I didn't really used to do a lot. It wasn't regular but in secondary school I went to church regularly. (Robert)

Group members also participated in church clubs.

The church I attended had a youth club and so every week we would go there. That was quite good. We used to do things like musicals and plays. We made a record and all sorts of different things. It wasn't simply table tennis. (Dionne)

Most Perseverers attended church but only two were actively involved in their church and its clubs.

Music tuition

Music lessons were undertaken by 67 per cent of the Perseverers while they were at secondary school. But as with church and its clubs, levels of involvement varied.

I had a violin which I never practised I never got on with that. Then I had piano lessons. I never practised. That was my fault. (Chantelle)

> I started music lessons when I was about 9 and I progressed to a different teacher and I continued until I was about probably 15 or 16 something like that. I got a grade two I think. (Dionne).

> During secondary school I was learning to play the treble guitar. So I did that for a while and then I got bored of it. Yes I was working towards grades and I did it for about a year really. (Samuel)

These experiences were typical: music lessons were generally not sustained but were short lived or not rewarding enough to encourage the practise needed to become competent musicians.

Other activities

Fewer Perseverers than High Fliers were involved in sports or youth clubs after school. Few visited museums but 29 per cent regularly used the library.

Of those who were interviewed, two were involved in sports clubs and one in a youth club. Marcus was responsible for setting up a local community club:

> I started my own community club, my own community centre at about 15 or 16. It was like organising facilities for young people in the area. I was running that for years. I was about 15, I think. Yes it took a lot of my time, I think. Most of the children that did come were Black but it was for anybody in the area to come. (Marcus)

Most Perseverers, however, said little about the quality of their activities and did not describe these experiences as rewarding or constructive.

Motivators and role models

Half the Perseverers said they had role models or mentors. These were members of the churches they attended.

> The person that really helped me was the minister of the church. He helped me but he had a heart attack and died. I didn't really appreciate his help until he had died. (Chantelle)

> There is one particular woman who to this day is very close to me. She was one of the first people to ever show an interest in a child.

> She would sit and talk to the children rather than adults who some-times would have a conversation that could go on above your head, but she was really interested in the individual children. She made an impact on me because she sent me my first-ever letter. And I was I don't know 7 or 8 and I had got to church on time that day or for a couple of weeks and she noticed it and sent me a letter and so she has been a great influence. (Dionne)

> There was a teacher who was our choir leader and obviously from church and was quite a role model. He was a very good motivator, because he would ask questions and give advice. (Samuel)

Role models within the community were an important aspect of these individuals' lives. More role models were reported by the High Fliers, Retakers and the Perseverers groups than the others.

School

Most Perseverers (64%) attended comprehensive schools while 29 per cent went to church schools. Positive feelings were ex-pressed about school but they also recounted many unpleasant experiences. The educational experiences they described were more like those of the Underachievers group than the High Fliers group.

School ethos

The Perseverers generally described their schools as having a positive ethos, but these descriptions were by no means straight-forward. Individuals spoke perceptively about the contrast be-tween the stated school ethos and the actual day-to-day teach-ing:

> The ethos, they wanted you to be hard working but to be honest when you look at the teachers most of them were 'has beens'. They didn't hack it in other schools. They got kicked out of the other schools and they came to the school I was going to. (Marcus)

> There was an element that if you worked hard you could succeed. There was that kind of ethos there. However, some teachers didn't give you that kind of encouragement. (Samuel)

The impact of a positive school ethos is inevitably dependent upon its execution in the relationship between teacher and pupil, as Marcus and Samuel were aware. Both recognised the failure of teachers to promote the positive ethos of the school with individual pupils.

Robert attended two secondary schools and said this about the second:

> No, I remember picking up positive messages about doing well and working hard. It wasn't even there in the first school I went to. (Robert)

So reflection made the group realise the presence or absence of positive encouragement and support and the related ethos of the school.

Teachers and teaching

Most Perseverers described teachers and the learning experience in negative terms but could remember exceptions who were positive and empowering and 'good'. When describing the teachers at her first secondary school, Dionne said

> I had good experiences and bad experiences on the whole. But looking back at that time I don't think that I was pushed very much. I remember the teacher saying to my mum that I wasn't capable of taking O-levels and that I wouldn't do very well in CSEs. I proved them wrong with that. But they weren't behind me with regards to the work. I felt that there wasn't much encouragement coming from the teachers. They didn't expect very much.

Lack of encouragement and low expectations were evident in other accounts:

> Most of the teachers were fine because as far as they were concerned there was this Black boy he can do well. Some of them had written me off because I think there were streams. There were six classes in our year and I started in the third stream. By the time I got to the fourth year I had moved up to the top stream. But then, that's when I saw the change in the teachers. They didn't want me in the class. I think it was only me and one other Black boy within that class

at the time. I noticed that they wasn't bothered with me. You know I am not supposed to be there. And that's how I was treated in those latter year. (Marcus)

Marcus described how after this his final years of school progressed with an intensification of racism and his growing awareness of it.

My experience of the last two years? That's where I believe I saw racism – in those last two years. Because you saw that you were never treated like anybody else. You were never encouraged, you were never encouraged at all in those final two years. Encouragement wasn't there and to be honest I remember when I took the mocks I think I got the top mock exam rates out of most of the classes and they was so shocked.

Marcus describes being promoted through the streams to find that on reaching the top stream, no encouragement or support were forthcoming. This contributed ultimately to his failure in school exams. Others had general difficulties in the school:

But what it was I think it was the way it was taught. There were a lot of Black people in there, a lot of people were rude in there. There was no form of discipline. I don't think the teachers could rule. And there were only Black children in school. It was like a black area and I think they couldn't really handle the children properly. So they just gave up and had like an attitude: well I'm teaching and if you wanna learn then that was it. (Robert)

The teachers who could not manage the Black children were in the majority in the school. The teachers' failure to control pupils and their consequent attitude towards teaching affected one Perseverer differently:

Some of them were all right I guess, they just delivered the lesson, they gave you homework. (Chantelle)

Receiving no more than 'delivery of the lesson' resonates with Robert's experience of teachers reaching a point where they simply taught the subject without regard for whether pupils were

77

learning. However, some of the Perseverers had teachers who were helpful. Dionne described in glowing terms the teachers at the secondary school she attended from aged 14:

> That for me was wonderful. That was one of the blessings of going there because the teachers were Black and that was positive for me to have positive role models. They were young, not much older than me. So it was good for me to see people I could look up to that had achieved degrees and stuff like that. At that time I don't remember knowing a lot of people who had actually done that. But they were really willing to do so much to get me through, to get us through. And I feel it was the complete opposite – instead of people saying, 'Oh you can't' for once in my life they were saying 'Well you can, you can achieve anything you want'. (Dionne)

Dionne's experience at her second school contrasted starkly with her first school with its message of 'you can't'. Other Perseverers could name a certain teacher who took the time to encourage and understand them:

> I had lots of problems at home which I guess would reflect on my studies. One teacher picked it up and I guess she thought it was neglect by my parents but I don't know but that wasn't until the fifth year. She was the one that actually encouraged me to get this job. (Chantelle)

> The PE teacher because he always pushed you to do more like when you ran for a mile you wanted to collapse but he kept you going. You know he was always very challenging. He used to push us all the time so that encouraged us in other things as well. So we felt motivated he made us feel like we could do something. And he used to give us certificates for achievements in even the smallest of things. (Samuel)

Certain teachers, then, were positive in their support and encouragement, but there were many accounts of negative and discouraging experiences with teachers. The teaching experiences of the Perseverers were principally negative with a few highlighting one or two positive teachers. But these were the exception.

These reports are similar to those of the Retakers and the Careerists who gave few accounts of positive teachers and teaching. In contrast, the High Fliers had largely positive and constructive experiences with their teachers.

Attitude towards school

Only 36 per cent of the whole group reported positive feelings about their secondary school experiences, less than at primary school where half the respondents had positive feelings. More Perseverers reported negative feelings towards school during secondary school. However, most of the Perseverers indicated that they had positive feelings about school.

> I went to a girl's school that was my first secondary school. I went there when I was 14. I really enjoyed it. It was a good school but then a new school opened and the last few months of my time at my old school were not as happy as I would have liked. So the opportunity came to leave. I was given the choice whether I would like to go to the new school or not. My younger brother automatically went there but I was given the choice. I thought I'll go. And I enjoyed it, I really did. (Dionne)

> I enjoyed some of the sports, the education, some parts of history, geography and music. Before I left school I wanted to be a recording engineer. At school we had our own recording studio and I would go down there. I liked working with tapes so I really wanted to do that. Running for my school that was a source of pride. (Isaac)

Although positive feelings were expressed about school, some accounts were not that positive. Marcus, for instance, said this about his success in his mock exams:

> I think secondary school was a wasted opportunity for me. And I think, okay, if I went to a better school they probably would have sorted me out as soon as they found I had that potential doing the mock exam. I believe at a better school I would have been looked after better and something would have happened. (Marcus)

79

Even though Marcus perceived school as a wasted opportunity he enjoyed it despite the difficulties he experienced. Robert also enjoyed school, but spoke about the boredom:

> When I started I really liked it but when I got to the fifth year I think I started to feel a bit bored. I played truant a few times at school because I was just like getting bored of it. But it was ok. It was alright but it could have been a lot better. (Robert)

Chantelle clearly disliked her school experiences, when looking back she associated it with other difficulties she was having at home:

> I would say that I wouldn't like to go through my experience again because I hated school. I hated the lessons. I guess maybe it reflected my home life because I hated my home life.

So although Perseverers were positive about their schooling any negative feelings were strong and lasting.

Unpleasant and negative experiences at school

The positive feelings expressed by the group, although general in nature, did not always take account of the unpleasant experiences many had had. Descriptions varied but generally pointed to a failure by teachers to support and draw each child towards meeting their full potential.

> I think I probably had some sort of dyslexic problem and if somebody had recognised that... in my day it wasn't even heard of. But probably if I had extra tuition; but the teachers didn't know I was struggling. Nobody knew so I just struggled along. (Chantelle)

Chantelle related how her school did not discover that she could not read until after her ninth birthday. Dionne describes an incident at school which remains with her today, when pupils told her that her father had died – when this was untrue. During this time she did not feel supported by the school:

> ... I never said anything to anybody, it sort of came out at the end of the day when I broke down. And one of the teachers didn't actually

believe me but once it was investigated they knew the girls once I described them. I didn't know them. They knew who the girls were but I don't know if any punishment was dealt out. My mother obviously was down at the school. My mother was sufficiently satisfied and at least we'd been heard. But I don't know if any action was taken. (Dionne)

Samuel described his fear of an intimidating and bullying teacher:

We had a French teacher who was quite aggressive in his attitude towards the Black children, the Black boys in the class. Most of the class were really frightened of him. Like he would shout and he was a bit of a bully, I would say. And so the students wouldn't stand for it and one particular boy who was very confident didn't do as he said... Basically the child was sitting at the desk and he came over to the child and pulled the desk up and pushed the child's head against the desk like that and then he pushed the table down and his fingers were there at the time. But I think at that time they realised that the teacher was out of order. The teacher realised that he had gone too far. He got dismissed. (Samuel)

Exclusion and truancy from school

Only one Perseverer had a formal fixed term exclusion from secondary school, but others experienced informal exclusion by being sent home from school – more than in the other achievement groups. The Perseverers also had the highest incidence of truancy of all the groups. Thirty six percent admitted to truanting from school while 43 per cent skipped particular classes. There are echoes of discontent about the exclusion experience and the way it was dealt with in this account by Marcus:

It was outside school hours. I went to the park and there was a funfair there. There was another White guy from our school. I saw him and he was with all his skinhead friends and Teddy boys, whatever. So he had a joke or something. We normally get on well and he was swearing and cursing and I thought what was going on? He was giving a lot of verbal to be honest. I said OK, we'll meet later on. So when we got back to school we had a punch up, he came out worse than I did.

> It so happened that I didn't come to school the next day and when I went back they said to me, 'You're going to be excluded from school for good'. So I said 'Why?' and they said, 'Because of the incident that happened yesterday outside school.' And I said, 'You haven't heard my version yet'. Then I had to go home, my parents came up after that. They said, 'You are going to be excluded.' 'But if I'm going to be excluded he must be excluded as well because we've both had a punch up together and if I came out worse would he be excluded?' They could not say anything. So when I brought that argument then they changed their minds, I wasn't excluded. (Marcus)

Marcus was unhappy with the way the school dealt with him. Although, not formally excluded, he was sent home from school and had to defend his position and challenge the school in order to avoid formal exclusion.

Robert was excluded from school on numerous occasions. He accepts that his behaviour often warranted such treatment but he argues that this was not always the case.

> I think on some occasions I did deserve to be suspended, on some occasions no, I didn't deserve to be suspended. When I was bored I used to do things like put the scissors in the drawer and just like, bend it and break it and stuff like that. And you know I used to get suspended for things like that. I would go in the cabinet sometimes I would go in the cabinet and just take it [scissors] because I was bored and like I was young and did stupid things like that. And other occasions when I used to get blamed for things which was not me and then I'd get suspended. I would have to stay at home for about a week. And then I'd be back in school. (Robert)

Robert's frequent exclusions were always for a fixed term. It seemed that his teachers did not explore the reasons for his behaviour. He described his behaviour as the result of keeping bad company, boredom and the poor discipline in the school.

> I was being naughty. I think I was being led by bad company. It was because I was bored I got all the laughs in school. Some of the classes you know I didn't really like... There was a maths class; the guy was called Mr Smith. He was very good, very strict, he was very

good. And there was another teacher an English woman; she was very strict too she was very good, you know, she wouldn't take any messing about. You had to read out in class and you had to do essays and everything. But I think it was the ones where they weren't so strict for some reason I just played up because I think I knew I could get away with playing up. (Robert)

Robert recalls two teachers who were strict and that he liked their classes, possibly because he came from a very strict home. Although this did not affect his behaviour at school, he may have felt more secure in a stricter classroom environment than a lax one. It also highlights the importance of teachers using robust behaviour management strategies.

Qualifications

The Perseverers held a range of qualifications including GCSEs, vocational and higher academic qualifications. All had Bachelors degrees except for one who had a Masters degree and a BTEC/ HND vocational qualification. Over half of the group (57%) had Bachelors degrees as their highest qualification while 36 per cent had Masters Degrees.

Reasons for exam failure

A large percentage (79%) of the Perseverers indicated that school was a factor in their lack of academic achievement more than any other group. Interviewees particularly stressed that teachers were not supportive and gave them no encouragement to study.

Over half (57%) of the group suggested that home was a factor in poor school performance, particularly the lack of support from parents. This, too, was higher than for the other achievement groups.

Seventy-one percent of the group said that their failure was due to personal characteristics. Not being motivated and not being interested in school were the two main factors cited. The Perseverers, more than any other group, stated that they were not interested in school. Thus the reasons for their underachievement at the end of secondary school, while mainly caused by school factors was due also to family factors and their own behaviour as pupils.

The achievements of the Perseverers were realised many years after they left school. In some cases, they were owed to the key messages of support and encouragement they received from parents, who despite their own low levels of education, lack of practical skills and time to invest in helping their children with their school learning, were keen to encourage them. The Perseverers experienced mixed interactions between the eco-systems of home, school and community and sometimes had contradictory experiences within them.

6

The Careerists

The Careerists held mainly vocational qualifications. Some had two or three GCSEs but did not qualify to be in any of the other achievement groups. Most were over 31 years old and again most were female (73%). The group made up 14 per cent of the whole sample and only three were interviewed. Just under half the Careerists were employed in skilled occupations and a further 27 per cent identified themselves as full time students.

Their parents' attitude to education

There was evidence that parents valued education (64%) but conditions at home for completing homework were not always conducive to study. The Careerists reported that their parents tried to motivate them but lacked the skills or knowledge to do so effectively. Parents were less educated than those of the High Fliers.

Of the three people interviewed, two recalled their parents valuing education. Martin had been sent to a private church school:

> What! They definitely wanted the best for me... and that's apparent because they were willing to pay for my education. That's why they sent me there, you know they wanted the best for me and they sacrificed in terms of money because the schools were really expensive. (Martin)

Despite, or perhaps because of, the efforts of these parents in their search for the best education for their son, they changed his school four times during his secondary years.

Shanice found that although her parents were not always explicit, their message was clear.

> Very, very supportive. It was their first priority. I know that's their way of being brought up. It wasn't that they were very explicit about it but 'without knowledge', they used to tell us, 'it opens all the doors for you. Education gets you everything.' It is the basic rudiments; you know a part of your daily life. You have to undertake it like everything else really. What you put in is what you get out. (Shanice)

However, not all the parents gave practical support:

> They wanted me to study when I got home. I don't think, sometimes they went the right way about it. (Martin)

> My parents weren't really interested in how I did at school. (Gabrielle)

The help parents gave was inconsistent and not always effectively delivered, possibly because of their own poor education. Less than 20 per cent of the mothers and fathers had had secondary education and only one (mother) had attended Further Education College. But the Careerists, more than any other group, did not respond to the question about parent's education level. Unlike over a third of the mothers, nearly one third of fathers were employed in manual occupations and none in professional or associate professional occupations.

Homework and routines

Fifty five percent of the Careerists reported having help with homework during primary and secondary school whether from members of their family, parents or a tutor. But 46 per cent reported that they throughout their schooling never had help with homework.

The three interviewees said they had not completed homework as regularly or routinely as the High Fliers had. Two reported completing homework but only one did so as part of a routine at home:

> I tried my best in the homework, but when you sat down in front of the TV and I was having my hair plaited and he [dad] was making you do your times tables, you're more likely to feel the pain of your hair being plaited than to think about the maths your dad set you. (Gabrielle)

> It was 50-50. It's hard to say. Different schools, you know, sometimes I did sometimes I didn't... The reason why I say that is because in fifth year we got homework but it was never checked.... But it was just my parents you know they were always arguing about whether it was right or wrong so I should have just done it myself. But my parents were willing to help if I asked them. (Martin)

These two Careerists both describe having to do their homework in distracting circumstances. Shanice struggled to concentrate on her work while coping with the discomfort of having her hair plaited. Martin watched his parents argue over the accuracy of his work. There was only one interviewee who had constructive help with homework, and in a way that was part of a set routine.

> He didn't necessarily give us work to do at home, but he oversaw the homework that we had from school... Yes, I had a set routine when we came in from school. The routine was basically, you came in from school, you changed because my mum has this thing where you don't play around in the same school clothes, you change your school clothes. And you put your home clothes on. Then you get something to eat, then if you've got any homework, and that's first priority, you do that. (Shanice)

Problems at home

Only one person in this group described the problems she faced at home.

> You can treat one child one way and another child a different way. I don't think I should have been beaten by my father. My father had problems that hadn't been dealt with and I think that if he had counselling or help, if that had been there for my dad, things would have been a lot easier... I didn't feel settled the way my dad disciplined us,

> my sister and I. That didn't help my learning and it made me some-
> times nervous. (Gabrielle)

The physical punishment she experienced contributed to a feeling of insecurity and injustice that inevitably impacted upon her
education.

Individual
Motivation

Although the Careerists talked about their motivation as adults,
they seldom mentioned any specific factor that influenced their
motivation during their school years. When commenting on her
change in self-motivation, Gabrielle described it as being pressure from her father:

> I think what used to motivate me before was basically pressure from
> my dad ... when I was growing up.

Others in the group spoke of their motivation only once they became adults:

> What motivates me is encouragement, support and success when I
> do something and it comes off really well. (Martin)

> In terms of what I've done and what I've been doing, I think, just
> always keep at the back of your mind what you want and don't steer
> away from that. (Shanice)

Thus it was only as adults that most of the Careerists became self
motivated.

Community
Church and church clubs

Just over half the sample attended church services during secondary school. During primary school 36 per cent were involved in
church clubs, falling to 18 per cent at secondary school. The three
Careerists who were interviewed had all attended church and its
clubs. And only one of these described being involved in church
services also. The others did not elaborate on their experiences.

Music tuition

Music tuition was common. Over half (55%) had lessons while at secondary school. Two said they had music tuition but this did not appear to be sustained: one spoke about having 'a bit of music lessons' (Martin) or 'a little bit of music lessons' (Shanice). They took no graded exams and the lessons did not continue for long.

Other activities

During secondary school over a third of Careerists were involved in sports club activities and just under a half attended youth clubs. Few visited museums regularly but a similar proportion to the High Fliers (46%) used public libraries.

All three interviewees participated in out of school activities. The two girls went to dance classes. One found that this became unpleasant when she moved from the inner city to a predominately White suburb:

> I did do modern tap and dance and that was when I was living in the urban city. But when I moved up to the suburbs they just made me feel uncomfortable about dancing... I was quite big and I wasn't happy with myself and the teacher was horrible to me even though I thought I did quite well. I still felt uncomfortable in that environment and I didn't have many friends. (Gabrielle)

One of the two interviewees who had engaged in sporting activities reported that this was not enjoyable because of the pressure:

> Yes, I got involved with sports outside of school. It was any form of what was going on, maybe running or badminton. I think I rebelled in a way because I was pushed so much into concentrating on the running, that even with the running, it wasn't good enough. (Shanice)

Careerists were less active in community activities than the academically successful groups and the experiences they had were not described as enjoyable, positive or consistent.

The Careerists did not have role models within the community.

School

This group expressed more negative feelings than positive towards school. Actual experiences of school were mixed. Some highlighted the lack of support from teachers. Most of the group attended comprehensive schools (73%). One (9%) attended a private school and one (9%) a church school.

School ethos

Only one Careerist claimed to have attended a 'good' school. Shanice attended what she professed to be a good school, but thought it was too relaxed:

> The school had a fairly good reputation... sort of okay, very pleasing very relaxing, but too relaxing. Too relaxing in the fact that if I didn't want to go to that lesson I could get away with it, which I didn't like. I felt that they should have had strict control class to class. I felt that if anyone gave any lame excuse they would get away with it. And I felt that that was not good enough. (Shanice)

The lack of discipline at school may have worked against Shanice achieving her potential. Martin changed secondary school four times and was educated for two terms in an American school.

> I went to a lot of schools. The school I went to- they pushed you, I mean when I was in America they pushed for you to do well. One which was the Black Christian school over here, they pushed for you to achieve well in life. I remember achieve in life, aim high. (Martin)

Gabrielle attended an average school which she described as 'an okay school'.

Attitudes towards school

The Careerists expressed more negative than positive attitudes towards both primary and secondary school. Positive attitudes towards primary school were expressed by nearly one third (27%) of the respondents but this fell to only 18 per cent for secondary school. Thirty six percent had negative attitudes towards both sectors.

Teachers and teaching

The Careerists had similar experiences to the Retakers with regard to their teachers and teaching. Gabrielle gave this account of her teachers:

> When it came to Art, even though I was good, the Art teacher that I had wasn't very encouraging, I didn't have any enthusiasm. One art teacher who was a supply teacher came and said that my work was good and my usual Art teacher didn't take any notice. I think they judged me based on my sister ... they said, 'Oh we know who your sister is.' I felt awkward and I didn't know what do. When new teachers came along they were quite good and they were encouraging but I think that the damage was done. By that time there was one teacher – my textile teacher – who encouraged me. (Gabrielle)

So Gabrielle could remember only one teacher who was encouraging. Otherwise she was judged by her sister's behaviour rather than on her own merit. Martin said about the secondary schools he attended:

> I remember sometimes there were teachers that I thought were not that good. Maybe they didn't spend the time that they needed with you, but I don't think enough attention was keyed in at school in your work.

Shanice was critical:

> But the only thing I found that was lacking in the school was the teachers themselves. Although they taught you the lessons, they taught you the lesson in a very I don't know if mundane or routine is the word, but what went on whether it was being disruptive or whatever they basically shunned that off and just wanted to get the work done...The teachers were all very old and not flexible. They were willing to get involved but I just found that they didn't understand. I saw that most were so into their routine, school routine. If anything, nothing was going to change, they were stuck. (Shanice)

The Careerists did not describe their teachers as good. The lack of attention, as identified by Martin, and the inflexible teaching methods Shanice found in her school negatively affected their schooling.

Unpleasant experiences

One Careerist had negative experiences at school and one was positive about school. When asked if she had had unpleasant experiences Shanice said:

> No, not really, I mean you get the odd things where you have an argument with all of the girls at school or something... But in terms of school when I think back it was good in that aspect, everything was fine.

She said she 'liked' school. Martin, the only man in the group, described his feelings about the three schools he attended during his secondary years:

> It was up and down. I would say like the first school that was like a thrill. And America was great and the last school was, academically, it was poor.

He changed secondary school because his parents moved him around when they were unhappy with his performance. He compares his experience in his American school with schooling in the UK.

> Thinking about it now I think I went to America and I got educated, I got educated. When I went to school over here I learned, I was taught, it was like this is the routine, the format and you just had to pick it up. But in America I got educated and that's deep because I learned things that I never knew about. (Martin)

Changing schools made Martin feel less positive about school but also exposed him to different styles of education. Gabrielle described her unhappiness at school when she moved into a new neighbourhood:

> I didn't enjoy school and I felt like an outcast, I didn't feel all that unhappy in my old school. I was happy and I was enjoying myself and I had fun. I went to ballet class out of school and when I went to Special school I enjoyed it. I felt very pressured and I went to the second special school and I felt uncomfortable and I didn't enjoy it as much as I wanted to I learnt a lot but I still felt a bit behind...

Gabrielle talks about being teased and how this affected the way she saw herself:

> I was not really bullied but teased and spat at. I felt uncomfortable with myself because when I was there I was teased a lot because I had quite a big bust and I was given a nickname. I was given a nick-name and I wasn't happy with myself and I hated the way that I looked so I didn't enjoy it. I got into sports and I liked it but I felt hor-rible because I was growing.

Gabrielle was bullied at school even if she did not recognise the fact. Thus the school experiences of this small group were mixed.

Exclusion and truancy

None of the Careerists experienced either fixed term or per-manent exclusion and none were sent home from school. Twenty seven percent experienced informal exclusion and were made to work away from their class for a day or more. There were no accounts of truancy or skipping classes among the Careerists.

Qualifications

The Careerists had vocational qualifications only. They did hold some GCSEs but nearly one third had only one. Most of the group (64%) achieved NVQs (National Vocational Qualifications), while 27 per cent (3) had BTEC/HND (Business and Technology Educa-tion Council/Higher National Diploma) certificates. Figure 6.1 on page 94 shows the highest qualifications they attained.

Reasons for failure at exams

The Careerists attributed their failure in the final secondary school exams to school and individual factors. Their reasons spanned all three ecosystems: home, school and personal. Of school factors, 'teachers not being supportive' was dominant, with 27 per cent reporting this. A few cited home factors such as unsupportive parents or family and one said that the home environment was not conducive to studying. The largest number of responses related to personal characteristics. Eighteen per

Figure 6.1: Highest qualification attained by the Careerists

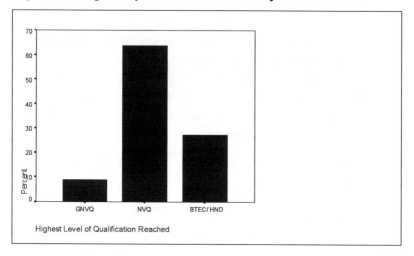

cent said that they had Special Educational Needs and 27 per cent that they lacked motivation at school. The Careerists had no overall pattern of positive experience across the ecosystems of home, school and community with which they interacted.

7

The Underachievers

The Underachievers comprised 14 individuals. Some attained a few GCSEs but over half the group had no qualifications at all. They were mostly over 31 years old and almost half were over 36. Most were women. Half the group were employed in skilled occupations and two said they were students. Most of them (71%) went into employment immediately after leaving school. The Underachievers made up 18 per cent (14) of the whole sample and five were interviewed.

At home
The parents' attitude to education
Less than half the group indicated that their mothers had positive attitudes to education – indeed two mothers' attitudes were described as negative – and just over one third of fathers valued it. But there was a high number of non-responses to this question. Perhaps this group had been aware of their parents' attitudes or perhaps their parents were not consistently present during their childhood. Or the participants may have considered the question to be irrelevant and so did not answer it.

Although some of the parents valued education, most of the group (60%) reported that their parents did not succeed in translating this into positive, effective, practical help and support. Janette said sarcastically:

> Oh yes! Education was everything. It was the most important thing and we didn't know how lucky were... And then you've got your mother, through our dysfunctional relationship, telling you that you are not going to be anything or whatever.

Janette went on to talk about her mother's negative expectations: 'She'd always said I wasn't going to be anything, or get anywhere'.

Clearly this woman had received mixed messages during her schooling. These messages affected her performance in academic work and her behaviour at home and school. Though she was made aware that education was important, she received no practical help or support.

Giving practical help

Forty percent of the Underachievers reported receiving support and encouragement from their parents, but some had reservations about its effectiveness:

> They would sit down and help with my homework and they would also give verbal encouragement... but because at church we had to go to conventions a lot ... you had to do your homework on the coach and things like that. Because it was like you have to be there all the time at the convention. That was the whole weekend and I used to think that was a bit unfair because I had to try and revise on the coach. (Daniella)

> Dad wanted us to do well but he never really spent the time that it really needs with the child for them to do well. He would say 'go and read a book' but not 'Let me sit down with you and go through it with you.' He never ever came to parents evening, it was always my mum that would come and she would try to encourage us all or reprimand us. (Davina)

On the whole parents gave little practical help and some even made it difficult for their children to undertake independent study effectively. Their own levels of education and employment may have been a factor. The questionnaire data revealed that over one third of mothers had been educated to secondary level and one to degree level, although one mother had received no formal education at all. But 21 per cent of fathers had only reached the level of secondary school. One respondent did not know the level of education reached by their father and one father was reported to have no education. Half the group offered no information about their parents' education. The reasons were unclear but it might be because they simply did not know.

Parents were employed in low level occupations, with only 21 per cent of mothers in associate professional jobs, the rest working in manual or skilled occupations. Again the question went unanswered for about 29 per cent of mothers and 43 per cent of fathers.

Homework and routines

Most of the Underachievers received no help with homework. Although 60 per cent reported completing homework, less than 40 per cent said this was as part of a routine at home. Although there was evidence of parental encouragement the constructive practical help to assist in completing it was lacking:

> Generally, father never had the time to spend with you to go through stuff. It's like you were told, 'Have you done your homework?' and stuff like that. But if you haven't got the understanding about what you are doing, then I found it was very difficult. (Desmond)

One respondent could not remember whether she even had homework, whereas Paula had had a lot of help and support with homework and this was part of the routine at home:

> Yes there was homework, then housework, but you had to do your chores. You have to do your homework, and then you have to do your chores, even if it meant doing your chores at 11 o'clock at night. You had to get your homework done. (Paula)

Other members of this group described having chores to complete, along with other regular evening activities such as dinner, TV and going out, but homework was not part of their routine.

Half the Underachievers had no help with homework during primary school. Of the remainder 21 per cent were given help by their parents. During secondary school, 43 per cent had no help whatever. Those who did reported that it came from parents, older siblings, friends and teachers.

Distrust of the school system

Only one person in this group reported parents' lack of trust in the education system. Most had appeared satisfied with the school system:

> She generally looked at the school report more than anything else, and she was quite satisfied with the comments that were made. That was enough for her. (Desmond)

> No, I think they were generally quite pleased with the choices of school and in terms of the teaching they were quite happy. (Daniella)

Their parents either saw teachers as always being right or had no contact with what went on in school except through their children's school reports.

Family and relatives as motivators

Two individuals described being motivated by relatives:

> My motivation is just my parents and encouragement from church brethren. I really just wanted to make sure that I did well, because mum and dad didn't have that and I wanted better for myself. (Daniella)

Janette's school years were characterised by exclusion and interaction with social services and children's homes. However, in the final few terms in a new school, with a new foster mum who managed to motivate her, she saw exams as a challenge.

> I mean it was a challenge and I remember saying to my mum, my foster mum, I'm going to do this. I'm going to show them that if they had taken the time with me I can be a good student. And I was really, really proud when I got my CSE grade one in English, CSE grade two, biology three, chemistry and the others. And I got my GCSE grades C in English and I was just really proud.... (Janette)

Although there were accounts of motivators they were fewer than for the High Fliers.

Problems and difficulties

There were indications of lack of support from home and 60 per cent of the group reported having problems with their parents. Davina describes her father's lack of interest in her work and the problems in the home:

> At the time I thought it was because he [dad] wasn't interested. But as I grew older and where I am right now, I don't think it was because he wasn't interested. I just don't think he had the confidence. ...She [mum] would tell dad how we were doing. She tried to encourage us as best she could but she had a problem to be dealing with, you know. So they had a conflict between themselves. So you know they were sorting that out. Although they didn't try to show it to us we knew it was going on. And at the time we knew we picked up hints of it we knew as children more than they thought we did. (Davina)

Despite being aware, with hindsight, that there was more to her father's apparent lack of interest, Davina's progress and performance in academic work at the time might well have been affected. Janette had problems at school and at home:

> I had been expelled from one school which was my second but last secondary school and basically my mum just gave up hope. She said to me, 'Oh, you aren't trying. I don't see why I should bother. I'm not going to put myself out to try and find you a school or whatever. Basically go and find a job'. Well you know what I mean? Nobody's going to employ a 13 /14 year old. (Janette)

She goes on to describe the breakdown of the relationship with her mother

> I was bad and basically my mum just didn't want to fight anymore. Do you know what I mean? Maybe she didn't want to fight anymore or maybe she had just given up on me. This was the final thing now because I wasn't in school. How was I going to be anything or get anywhere? So I think she just gave up on me. She just could not be bothered – she had four other children and I'm the middle child.

As Janette's case illustrates, the impact of difficulties in the home can be devastating to children's education.

Individual characteristics
Motivation

The Underachievers were interested in their motivation now, and offered few descriptions of self-motivation when at school. Only one mentioned self motivation for academic achievement:

> I didn't have the same motivation [then]. It was different. This is a greater motivation. It's more now than that which was at school. There wasn't much motivation. I cannot look back and say I had a greater motivation at school. (Desmond)

Daniella was motivated to do office work and appeared always to have wanted this:

> But that was me from young. I've always wanted to do that, anyway. And that was why I really followed that sort of path. That was just what I wanted to do. (Daniella)

Self motivation seems to have increased when these participants became adults. Unlike the High Fliers, they showed no evidence that religious belief was a motivating factor.

Difficulties and problems

The Underachievers had difficulties related to home and school. Paula tells how she suffered intense anxiety when taking exams even though she worked hard:

> But I also had difficulties in exams. I mean, for one, my doctor gave me Valium. It was just in the exam setting. I just couldn't take the pressure. It was too much. There were quite a few kids that suffered from that, I think.

Community

Involvement in community activities was inconsistent and generally characterised by negative experiences. This group had fewer positive role models than the successful groups, and experienced more negative interactions within and between the ecosystems of the home, school and community.

Church and clubs

Sixty four percent of the Underachievers attended church services while at primary school but this dropped to 43 per cent at secondary level. Few were involved with church clubs. And they did not always actively participate, neither did they attend regularly. Desmond recalls being involved in the activities at church but only when activities had been arranged:

> It would depend if there was anything laid on by the church or anything like that. Then we would go. Then we would probably be involved in different activities there. (Desmond)

Paula's experience of church was also inconsistent and her parents did not attend:

> I had an aunt who used to go to church we went to her church, but we went to loads of different churches. My parents always insisted that we went to a church; they didn't care what church we went to. We went to a church, but they didn't come. A minibus used to come to pick us up and someone would bring us home, but they didn't go. (Paula)

Being sent to church with a relative may have given Paula the impression that church attendance was unimportant to her parents. Others did not enjoy attending church:

> We used to go to a Pentecostal Church. I didn't actually like it because it was a bit too 'happy, clappy' for me. It was a family church so you come in with your family from outside it was like there was just too much politics in it. As soon as it was time to leave I tried to get out and stop going. (Davina)

Close involvement such as setting out the chairs and leading out in services described by members of the other groups was not seen among the Underachievers. They attended erratically, were not engaged and seemed to have been forced to go.

Music tuition

Over one third took music lessons while at primary school but only 29 per cent did so at secondary school. Their accounts of learning to play an instrument were not always of a pleasant experience.

> My sister, she was forced to play the guitar and I was forced to play the guitar and subsequently I don't think either of us can play a key on it. We went for quite a while. It was private and then we used to have lessons at school as well. To be honest with you, I weren't really that keen on it. I'm the sort of person that if I'm going to be doing something it's got to be because I wanted to do it and not because somebody has forced me to do it. (Desmond)

One Underachiever who enjoyed her music lessons had them stopped as a punishment if she misbehaved.

> Basically, the only activity I did get to do, because I played the piano by ear and I played the piano at school. My sister told my mum about it and my mum arranged and had piano lessons for me and my sister. I didn't do grades I can play some things, I can read music and I can still play by ear. My lessons were stopped as a punishment. It was the one thing I enjoyed, it was one thing I looked forward to and it was the one way she could punish me. So when I was too naughty they got stopped. (Janette)

This group's parents gave no support for music tuition.

Other activities

Few Underachievers attended sports activities or youth clubs. Fourteen percent visited museums while in secondary school and 29 per cent regularly visited the library. Going to the library rather than a museum increased noticeably at secondary school. Overall, few of them participated in other out of school activities and their experience of other activities was infrequent and often negative.

> I was not allowed to go anywhere. Even when I came home from the children's home on holiday I was not allowed to go anywhere, unless I took my younger sister with me. (Janette)

Role models

Daniella and Paula both mentioned role models:

> Well, now my pastor. I first met him when I was about 13 or so. I sort of grew up knowing him. The pastor was really a mentor, because he always seemed to go for what he wanted and he has got it really. And he's very encouraging. (Daniella)

> Mayo Angelou, I read a lot of her stuff and I really admired everything she went through and yet she succeeded. This Black teacher, who's become a friend of the family he was a really good role model and then there are couple of people on TV people like Trevor Macdonald. Black people who were in positions that I saw as prominent were really kind of important to me and Black people that made people stand up and think like Nelson Mandela. (Paula)

Having a role model was significant for these two women but the group overall had fewer role models than the successful groups did.

School

All the Underachievers attended comprehensive schools. Few expressed positive feelings about their schools and it was this group who described the most negative experiences at school. They attributed their failure in examinations to a combination of unsupportive teachers, lack of general support, being excluded and their own lack of interest in education and motivation to do well.

School ethos

Forty percent of Underachievers described their schools as 'good', whereas others said they attended 'bad' schools. But closer examination showed that although the good schools appeared to have desirable reputations, their ethos and the messages they gave to students were questionable.

Desmond, who had his primary schooling in the Caribbean described the culture of the school there:

> It would be one of, you had to learn while you were there. There were no two ways about it. It never happened to me, but I know people who if you didn't make the grade, you just stayed there in the same year and so you had to make the grade it was like you were made to. You had this thing instilled in you that you had to learn you had to learn the necessities to make the grades... (Desmond)

He described his reaction on arriving in the UK and the culture shock he experienced attending a British school for the first time,

> It was very interesting it was a culture shock, just the different aspects of it really, coming up and going through the system here. To be honest with you, looking back at it now, I can say it's like going through the system; you are on a conveyor belt and going through the system. Start off at one point and as long as you reach the other end irrespective of how you reach it didn't seem to matter and that was the feeling that I got.

Two others in this group had changed schools and this affected them negatively, even though their new schools were perceived as good.

> I was beginning to get on really well, then we moved. Just coming up to the end of the third year and we moved and it was a completely different ball game. At that time they didn't have a national curriculum – they taught different things in different schools. So when I [arrived] I didn't understand what they were doing at all. The work was so completely different, it was different learning skills to what I was used to. I remember going there and having to sit for an exam I hadn't even studied for. It was terrible, it felt awful. And I just don't think I really recovered from that, not for a long time. I was there for the last two years of school. It wasn't very good because their whole teaching ethos was completely different and I just wasn't used to it so I never really caught up. (Davina)

Because of problems at home and at school, Janette described herself as having attended 'loads of secondary schools' some of which were reported to be 'good' and others that were not. She experienced numerous exclusions and spent time in social services care. She missed two whole years of schooling when permanently excluded and returned during the latter part of year nine. She missed the chance to experience a school ethos that encouraged excellence because of the difficulties she experienced at home and at school:

> Yeah I went to a school that was meant to be a very good school. But anybody who I went to school with I can't remember any of them saying that they had a good experience... (Janette)

Paula also attended a poor school:

> It was a streamed school and I was in the top stream. It had a bad reputation, I think because it was made from two modern schools and for no other reason.

Overall, the school experiences of the Underachievers were characterised by difficulties with adjusting to a new school or attending schools that lacked a positive and encouraging ethos. There was little evidence of their schools providing positive and encouraging learning environments.

Teachers and teaching

Negative incidents were experienced by many of the group particularly with teachers. The pattern was of unhelpful experiences with their teachers and scant support, although they gave some accounts of positive experiences with teachers. The older teachers seemed to relate to them differently, as some noted:

> If I can remember rightly, I'm not generalising now, but some of the teachers, their attitude was great. I think the ones that probably had problems were the older teachers. If I'm going to say there were any with any sort of reservations, it would be with the much older teachers. At the time they were quite good, pretty good, very supportive in my being a stranger in a strange place. Basically, they sort of tried to make you feel at ease in the environment. (Desmond)

> In the other school it was completely different. Because we had come from a city school I think the teachers already had set us aside as being troublemakers. I remember once the headteacher saying, 'You know this is a completely different ball game. We know that you come from an inner-city school, but you know we have different rules here.' And he was quite obnoxious and we would argue quite often. I didn't get on with him at all. There were one or two [teachers] that were very modern in their thinking, and I got on extremely well with them but the more traditional teachers I did not get on with at all. (Davina)

There were some indications of having understanding teachers but what remained with Davina was being stereotyped because she came from an inner-city school. Despite a catalogue of bad experiences in school, subsequent exclusions and attending several secondary schools, Janette found one head teacher who was willing to give her time.

> The only person that took an interest in me was Mrs H who was the headmistress. But none of the other teachers really bothered with me. The only other person in the school that did bother with me was my English teacher, who told me that my written English and my spoken English was much better than any of the children that she had in her classes and these were children who were born here. Obviously, they were all White students and she actually put me forward for the extra exam in which I got my GCSE. I got a C. The other teachers were not really interested. It was coming up to exam time and they had their little clutch of pupils who they knew would produce good grades and those who weren't going to. I hadn't been there long enough to do the course work that led up to these exams and so like there was gonna be no hope for me and they didn't put any effort into me. And when I understood something they were very surprised that I had any knowledge of it and if I didn't understand something they would get very frustrated and think this was a demonstration of the bad behaviour that they had been told about. (Janette)

Paula had negative interactions with teachers and the familiar problem of being pushed into sport:

Oh yes, one of our teachers was dismissed because he had a lot of National Front stuff sent to the school. One of the boys in our school, a teacher threw a blackboard eraser at him and he lost the sight in one eye, so that was going on. And it was all brushed under the carpet. And we also had a teacher who was eventually dismissed for sexually harassing the girls. Me, I would go into the class and he'd be counting the girls and he would say you count for two, looking at my boobs and stuff like that. So with those things going on, for the other Black kids, it was tough, you know, it was very tough. And the other thing, we were always pushed into sport. You know Black kids can run, Black kids can do this, we were always pushed into sports. There were trips out and the White kids would always get to do the really classy things and we were always doing running. (Paula)

The Underachievers described more negative school experiences than those in other groups. School was characterised overall by negative and discouraging teachers, although there were a few exceptions.

Attitudes towards school

The Underachievers had the highest number (36%) of all the groups who reported that they had negative attitudes towards primary school: only 14 per cent reported feeling positive about it. For secondary school only 36 per cent reported feeling positive.

Unpleasant experiences

The Underachievers had the most negative experiences (80%) although, with only five members, they were one of the smallest groups. The nature of the negative experiences varied. Two encountered racism from the other pupils. Davina encountered racial conflict in her new school and this troubled her:

The school that I came from, we had a really good mixture of children we got on so well and there [new school] the majority of children were predominately White. There were just a few Blacks there and Asians as well. And there was often conflict amongst children about colour bar and colour prejudice which to be honest I really didn't know anything about because I came from a really good mixed school. (Davina)

The only man in the group did not take on board the racism he experienced:

Here, basically, the only thing I can remember were the kids. You would hear them talking about golliwog and stuff like that. And basically, I would say 'What are you talking about?' and they would say to me 'You know the Black man on the jam jar'. And I would say, 'No'. But it carried on. To be honest really, it really didn't have any impact on me to that extent. I would answer to the person that if you don't like me, good luck to you. And I'm gone. So it really does not stand out as an unpleasant experience at all. (Desmond)

Other kinds of unpleasant experiences included bullying that could not easily be ignored:

For my first school it was bullying. But it wasn't bullying in the second school, it was teasing because we had a completely different accent as well so they would tease us about that... (Davina)

The school that we moved to it was horrible, absolutely horrible. We were constantly bullied by the other pupils and nothing was done about it. But in that school at the time there was another Black family. Both families had the same kind of treatment. But they were felt to be somewhat above us because they had two parents who were married and we were a single parent Black family. We were really looked down on by the teachers because obviously children wouldn't have access to that information. The teachers were really, really horrible to us and the children and whatever they did, it was an accident. If they hit us, it was an accident, if they called us a nasty name they are only trying to be friendly and trying to find a pet name for you. Do you know what I mean? It was like we had to accept this and the school wasn't going to do anything about it. (Janette)

Janette offered a whole catalogue of negative experiences in the different schools she attended. The teachers gave her no support. The abuse she suffered was from children but also from teachers:

> It was horrible. Horrible, we were constantly picked on and slapped. We used to have our hair plaited... and if we were naughty, the head-mistress would come and get us out of class and she would hold us by our topknot and yank us to her office, do you know what I mean? ...And she would come and get us out of the classroom and we'd be yanked in from in front of children so the children would see us being treated this way. So when we got into the playground it doesn't surprise me that they thought they could treat us that way as well. I mean we used to be slapped every day, I mean it was awful. You know what I mean – going home with people's handprints in our faces you know because we would answer back. We didn't know what we were doing wrong, we could not ever be good, we could not ever be right. (Janette)

Not all the group had such terrible memories of school but they did recall instances of unfair treatment:

> Actually it's quite strange because we took the 11 plus in our primary school and now my understanding is that I passed the 11 plus. There are only a limited number of places. I passed the 11 plus and my parents chose for me to go to a grammar school. However, there was a limited number of spaces in the grammar school. My parents told me that they were actually informed that although I passed the 11 plus they should understand that if there was a teacher's child for example who passed, that they would get the first go at the grammar school. (Paula)

When talking about motivation, Paula recollected her desire to be a teacher. But the way the school treated her made her feel that she was not good enough to be a teacher:

> I think school kind of knocked that out of me. I had always wanted to be a teacher and when I realised that I wasn't going to be a teacher and me looking back now I could have been, I could have sort of said and sort of gone in a different direction. But I didn't even think in that way, as I got it into my head that I wasn't good enough. I think that kind of career thing was knocked out of me.

Inevitably, having had such negative experiences meant this group had negative feelings about school:

> Not a very good experience at school. I don't look back and think; Oh I had very good experiences, school the best years of your life. I couldn't wait to leave. I don't think I had a very good experience. (Davina)

When asked about her feelings about her school experiences, Janette launched into a long account of incidents of mistreatment. But in the middle of relating these harrowing accounts she said:

> I wanted to be a teacher when I was in primary school and I was told 'You be a teacher? Never!' and I would come up with all this stuff and at that time I was under nine and I've got these people telling me how these things are nothing to do with me and nobody's gonna let you be a teacher. And then you get into secondary school and people are saying to you, well basically other than factory jobs there was no jobs for Black people and what is the point. Yes J. you are clever, you are exceptionally clever but at the end of the day nobody is going to give you a job and it's like what is the point? Why have you bothered to let me in the door? (Janette)

The impact of such negative messages can only be guessed at, but they certainly contributed to Janette's lack of achievement in school. Another held the school responsible for her lack of achievement.

> I feel that the school failed me because I had so much potential and with the support – I mean I did CSEs when I think I should have done O-levels. I was in the top stream there was no reason why I shouldn't have done O-levels. So I think the school failed me, in the sense that they didn't support me to reach my full potential. (Paula)

The sense of failure and being let down by school was strong, particularly for Paula, who should have achieved more because she was in the high ability group.

Exclusion and truancy

One Underachiever was permanently excluded in secondary school and 29 per cent experienced exclusion. Fourteen percent had been excluded for a fixed period. Twenty nine percent had experienced informal exclusions; either being made to work away from their class for more than a day or were sent home from school without being formally excluded. The group had 21 per cent who admitted to regularly truanting from school or skipping certain classes.

Janette, who experienced a number of permanent and fixed term exclusions, had difficulties both at home and school.

> By the time I was in the [second] school I was already in voluntary care, living in a children's home. So this is about the second year so that would have made me 13. I'd already had lots of problems at home and I'd run away and I was at the school, it was a very snobby school. It was one of the top grammar schools and they really didn't want me there and I got expelled from there because I could knit and they were going to teach me to knit. I said, 'can't I do crochet or something else?' But basically they said, 'The whole class is doing knitting, you have to do knitting'. Well I didn't want to do it but I had this teacher literally try to force me to pick up the needles. And of course it ended up with me fighting with the teacher and I got expelled. OK, fair enough. Then I was out of school for a while, for a long time. (Janette)

Janette missed most of her third and fourth year of secondary school. She described developing behavioural problems and being unable to settle at school. She described in detail two events that led to her being excluded again:

> I remember there was an exam sign up in the hall and if you rubbed it the letters went kind of silver. I was doing that and some male teacher hit me. And I ended up fighting with him because I had never been hit by a man in my life so I got suspended for a while. I went back and then this chemistry teacher went and slapped this White girl. Our PE teacher had to be rushed to hospital so we couldn't do PE. So this teacher was asked to take us but we enjoyed our PE lessons, we didn't want to go and do a chemistry lesson. This girl said 'I'm not doing it!' and this teacher, a White teacher, hit her so hard in her face and I said 'you can't do that!' And I said 'make sure you tell your parents', and this teacher came over and picked me up by my neck and had my feet off the floor and because I objected strenuously to being treated like that I got expelled.

> They wanted me to apologise to her and I said, 'not unless she apolo-gises to me.' And my mum took me to the school to make me apolo-gise and I said 'No, I am not apologising, Get a solicitor because you can't do that.' And I told my mum 'She can't do that to me I was gag-ging! She can't do that. The whole class saw it.' 'No solicitor's going to defend us.' She [mum] is saying this to me in front of the White headmaster. 'You think that with your black skin any White people's going to stand up and say they saw that White teacher hit you a Black child?' Basically she was saying you've got away with this because we are Black and I know there is no point in me going to get a solicitor to defend you because we are black, even though the law is there to defend us.

What is disturbing about these accounts is not just the level of force used by the teachers but that Janette's mother felt so dis-empowered and unable to get the support to ensure justice for her daughter. Her mother's perception of racism was strong enough for her to feel that no one would stand up for her Black child against a White teacher. And the headteacher appeared by his silence to confirm her conclusion.

Despite several exclusions, Janette went on to achieve a GCSE exam pass in English, encouraged by her teacher. This suggests that support and interest from teachers can help in enabling pupils to focus on their strengths.

Qualifications

This group was formed from those who had four or less GCSEs or equivalent on leaving school and no other specified qualifica-tions. One person had received work related training but had no GCSEs. Half of the group had none at all and only 21 per cent had four GCSEs. (See figure 7.1 opposite)

Reasons for exam failure

The Underachievers attributed their failure to achieve in exams to home, school and personal characteristics. The school factors they cited were: unsupportive teachers (21%), and that Black

Figure 7.1: Number of GCSEs Attained by the Underachievers

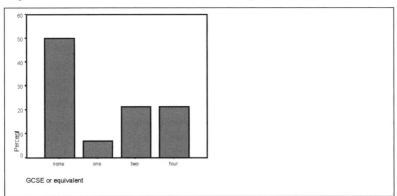

pupils were not encouraged to study. Only 14 per cent described their parents as supportive. The personal characteristics cited for failing in exams were: being excluded, not being interested in school and disliking the teachers. Twenty one percent said they were not motivated.

While there were exceptions, the Underachievers tended to be in negative and unsupportive environments within their home, school and community. They had fewer positive experiences overall than the other groups and this affected their ultimate school achievement.

8
Helping Eagles to Soar

The findings

The findings of my research highlight the importance of developing resilience in children, to enable them to cope with the challenges they face in school and out. The research suggests that the interactions between the participants and the various ecosystems in which they operate strongly affected their academic achievement. The largely positive and supportive childhood experiences the High Fliers had contributed to their academic success. Similarly, the broadly negative school experiences of the Underachievers and their lack of support contributed to their poor performance at school. There are, however, no simple explanations. The interacting factors that produce differential attainment are complex and interwoven. What is clear is that variations in individual, family, school and community conditions produced a variety of responses, behaviours and consequent attainment.

This book offers no more than a snapshot of some lived experiences but it illustrates the complexities of human nature, social interactions and reactions, and especially how these affect educational attainment. Other individuals in similar circumstances to the Underachievers, for example, might have developed resilience from some source and succeeded at school. The factors presented here do not even represent the entire experience of each respondent but only what they deemed important and relevant. And they may be applicable only to my sample – I do not claim that they are representative of all African Caribbeans in the UK. But the snapshots present a critical case which can help us understand the school experiences of Black children. Despite the relatively small sample the research has 'intuitive appeal' (Lee *et al,* 1991) and usefully adds to the research literature the interpretations and perceptions of Black people themselves about their schooling in Britain.

Eagles who Soar shifts the focus of research from underachieving Black pupils to those who are academically successful. This is not to ignore the needs of Black pupils who struggle in school and underachieve but to recognise that forty years of research and public focus on underachievement has served to feed the stereotype of Black pupils as underachievers. This book has sought to identify the factors which support Black pupils' academic success by exploring their experiences in the home, school and community and how these influenced their academic progress and attainment.

A significant contribution of this book is the evidence it provides for what the African Caribbean community has known for decades: that most of their children have negative encounters with staff and pupils, regardless of the type of school they attend or their own abilities. In their interactions with staff and pupils they experience varying degrees of difficulty and often feel unfairly treated and unsupported. The way Black pupils navigate their way through these negative experiences affects their academic success or failure. Those who are able to succeed and achieve academically at the end of secondary school do so because they have developed resilience outside of school. Affirmation and support at home and in the community are crucial to school success.

Challenges

All research has methodological limitations and this study is no exception. What matters is that the limitations are taken into account when drawing conclusions. The composition of the sample was an issue of concern for two reasons. Firstly, few respondents were unemployed and secondly, many of the respondents attended church. Although I targeted locations where the unemployed could be accessed, few responded. This means that the possibility of sample bias cannot be ruled out. That so many reported that they attended church during their school years might also be due to my targeting churches as one source for my sample. The high number of respondents with degrees or working towards degrees might also indicate sample bias. With the type of sampling used in this study it is possible that 'all kinds of unspecifiable biases and influences are likely to influence who gets sampled' (Robson, 2002, p265).

Another limitation of my research was the sample size. A low response rate generated only 78 questionnaire responses and 32 interviews. Consequently the findings cannot be generalised to the population of Black school children in the UK. Dividing the sample into achievement groups created a further difficulty, as most groups were scarcely of a size suitable for qualitative analysis: the Careerists had only three members and the Underachievers and Retakers five each. So the results should be regarded with caution. There is nevertheless value in the data and it is valid in that it represents the lived experiences of real individuals (Fife-Schaw, 1995).

Moreover, this study has targeted a larger sample of Black pupils than previous qualitative work in the field has done. It allows Black people to share their reflections on their experiences, perspectives and views of their journey through schooling. It captures the personal accounts of their experiences at home, school and in the community and describes their perceptions of what contributed to their educational attainment.

The difference

The differing childhood experiences of those who did well at school and those who did not illuminates the way community involvement supports success. Consistent and regular involvement was important and so was personal enjoyment. Community activities supplemented positive home environments, providing a locus for achievement oriented engagement and a strong network which enhanced the children's resilience. The church and its clubs played a part. So did the people who served as role models and gave consistent support. Participating regularly in music tuition and the enjoyment this gave enhanced the rewards for making an effort.

The homes of successful pupils were characterised by their parents' high expectations, encouragement, practical support, help with homework and active involvement with and understanding of school procedures. These parents contributed to their children's resilience so that home and community combined with individual factors such as motivation, self esteem and having clear goals. The resilience thus developed enabled these pupils to cope with negative experiences of school in ways that did not prevent their pursuit of excellence.

Understanding the importance of resilience for Black children casts light on the processes affecting their school achievement. This book raises the serious question of why Black children need to develop such resilience in order to achieve at school. It challenges the policies, practices and procedures adopted in schools which so affect these children that they need to protect themselves in order to survive and achieve.

The research also demonstrates how some Black communities and families manage to support their children appropriately while also challenging the negative processes inside the schools. Recent government policy encourages schools to work closely with parents and communities to generate links to improve the educational experiences of Black children (DfES, 2003 and DfEE,

2000). If implemented, they will support positive interactions between the pupils' ecosystems and enhance their chances of achieving their academic potential.

There are government initiatives that aim specifically to address the difficulties experienced by ethnic minority pupils and to improve achievement, such as the Ethnic Minority Achievement Grant, changes in the educational provision for excluded pupils and the Social Exclusion Unit (SEU). Studies by, among others, the Runnymede Trust (1998), Ofsted (Gillborn and Mirza, 2000), DfEE (Blair and Bourne, 1998; Cline *et al*, 2002), Race on the Agenda (Richardson and Wood, 1999), *Why Pick on Me?* (Blair, 2001) and the Commission for Racial Equality (1996), have investigated the issues affecting ethnic minorities and educational achievement and suggest ways for parents, teachers, governors and LEAs to respond. However, none seem to have effectively raised achievement amongst Black pupils relative to other groups, nor have they reduced the relative number of exclusions.

This book suggests a more holistic approach to improving achievement levels by addressing the interactions between the ecosystems that individuals operate within and which it has shown to so greatly affect their life chances. To change things for the better the community, both home and school need to be considered, along with each child's personal motivation and aspiration.

The way forward

If we really want to see Black children achieving to their full potential and truly becoming eagles then we all have a responsibility to respond in some way to the findings described in this book.

Parents

For more Black children to become High Fliers, the work begins in the home. In the parent workshop referred to in Chapter 2, parents reflected on some of the findings of this research and considered their own situations. They were asked to come up with three strategies they would implement in their homes at once to engender change and they suggested the following:

- leave work on time

- expect the best from my child

- give my children a sense of self worth

- include my children in family decisions

- give positive encouragement and praise

- network with other parents, family members and friends to ensure a strong support network

- communicate my expectations clearly

- share motivational quotes with my children, putting them up around the house.

This is just the beginning. It is time for parents to act collectively and come together to set up networks and support groups to share information and provide guidance and support for other parents who might lack confidence, knowledge or skills on how best to help their children with homework and school work. Support groups and networks that have developed through the supplementary school system could be used as a forum for making links with schools and learning about school processes and legislation. If parents can begin to see a way to change the home situation for their children by creating more supportive home environments their children are likely to develop greater resilience to the negative impact of racism in school. The collective strength of parents' groups can be utilised to make demands on schools and local authorities to improve the education provided for Black children.

The participants in this research shared their desire to see parents building confidence and self awareness in their children. They recognised that Black children need to have a strong sense of self worth and self esteem so they can cope in a predominately White society. They also suggested that there is a need for more input from parents in making their children aware of available career possibilities by exposing them to the wider world. Families should be strong and should provide a clear cultural identity. But it is not enough to expect the parents to change, as they too need support. This is where the Black community has responsibilities too.

The community

The Black community has a responsibility to provide activities that support children's achievement and self development, so helping to encourage Black children as they navigate the school system. There are a number of successful voluntary and community initiatives operating but many are poorly funded. The supplementary school system was not explicitly mentioned by the participants in this research. However, these schools set out to provide an education which celebrates Black heroes and their achievements in the context of an encouraging environment for Black children (Simon, 2005). Today many struggle to survive. Many of them are seeking government funding; others are trying to raise funds in order to remain independent.

Of particular importance are the Black churches which, as established organisations within the community, can provide an infrastructure to support mentoring programmes, liaison with schools, parents and supplementary education and various activities. They are well placed to provide additional help to families within their locality. David Simon (2005) suggests that Black churches with their 'loyal clientele, resources, self-reliance, and independence' (p70) could make it possible for supplementary schools to continue and flourish. Furthermore, local communities can seek government funding and pool resources so that effective activities and community initiatives can be offered on a permanent basis, rather than for the short term – too often the case for some excellent initiatives.

Schools

The Race Relations Amendment Act (2000) places a duty of care on all local authorities to eliminate unlawful racial discrimination and promote equality of opportunity and good relations between people of different racial groups. In addition to a specific race relations policy, schools must have in place strategies to raise educational attainment amongst ethnic minority pupils, promote equality of opportunity and build good relations between different racial groups. Schools have a responsibility to examine their policies and practices continually to ensure that they do not work against the interests of Black pupils.

Yet the disproportionate numbers of Black pupils being excluded from school in their final years of schooling persists, affecting their life chances. Large numbers of Black children are still failing at GCSE. This raises questions about teacher assessment, setting and banding and the tiered system of GCSE examinations.

Gillborn (2005) describes in detail the system whereby pupils are separated into bands which take different GCSE exam papers. This might at first seem acceptable but a closer look reveals that the higher tiered paper allows pupils to achieve A*-C grades but the lower tiered paper (sometimes referred to as the Foundation tier) restricts the highest grade that can be achieved to a C. In Mathematics there are often three tiers and pupils entered in the lowest can achieve no higher than a D grade which for most is not a pass but a fail. A system where pupils who work hard are being set up to fail cannot be right! If, as Gillborn's research suggests, the lowest sets or bands are comprised of the majority of Black pupils and based on teacher's judgements about which children are likely to achieve success in GCSE exams, it is little wonder that Black pupils continue to remain the lowest achieving of all groups. Where is the equality of opportunity in this system?

Teachers need additional training that makes them aware of the issues relating to the education of ethnic minority children and how certain influences and procedures in school can be damaging to their progress. Teachers must examine their own perceptions and stereotypes. Stereotyping is part of human nature (Tajfel, 1978; Hamilton and Rose, 1980) but stereotypical perceptions that work against certain groups of pupils still prevail, and must be challenged and overcome. Teachers also need training and guidance in conflict management. The impetus for change in schools must start with the headteacher.

The TDA (Teacher Development Agency) reports each year that most beginning teachers still feel inadequately prepared for teaching in diverse schools. The TDA should fund and monitor equality training programmes in all initial teacher education institutions. And the present inadequacy needs to be addressed through continuous professional development programmes for practitioners.

The Every Child Matters outcomes afford opportunities for schools to develop training sessions for parents so they can better provide educational support and guidance for their children as they enter each phase of schooling: nursery, primary and secondary. This would also allow communication about what parents expect from the school and what the school expects from parents and pupils. A useful discussion forum for guidance could be developed, about helping with homework and building links between the home and school.

Participants in my research had clear views about what schools could do to improve the situation for Black pupils. They suggested that the school curriculum needed to include more positive information about Black people and address the whole range of Black experience instead of focusing on slavery. They recommend that Geography cover the Caribbean so that all children learn that it is made up of more than just Jamaica. They recommend that History, while still covering slavery, should teach about the many Black soldiers who fought for Britain in the World Wars. In essence they recommend that the curriculum be more relevant and inclusive. They stressed the need for more Black teachers, better quality careers advice, more training for teachers in Black cultural awareness. They wanted teachers to be able and willing to spend time building relationships with Black pupils. A few of the participants spoke about the way that teachers see groups of Black pupils who congregate together in the school grounds as threatening gangs rather than as a group of friends, when similar groups of White pupils are regarded as harmless.

Government

It is usually only when government stipulates change that change at school level begins to happen. The government needs to do more about school exclusions and the disproportionately high level of exclusions of Black boys than merely publish and comment upon the dire exclusion figures. It needs to galvanise the agencies responsible to take effective action and make changes to ensure that the needs of those most at risk of exclusion are met and that wider issues affecting their lives and education are addressed. A start has been made by setting up the SEU and it is hoped that its recommendations will be implemented.

While there is a role for parents, communities and the schools in raising Black achievement there is also a role for government and government agencies. The government has the responsibility to ensure that initiatives implemented to reduce underachievement are supported by and founded upon research findings about Black pupils and their own experience of the educational system. Initiatives which prove successful need long term ring-fenced funding to ensure they continue.

The research community

It is imperative that the academic research community documents the experiences of successful Black people in Britain and maps their progress through the school system and the many obstacles and challenges they face. An increase in research of this type, which challenges preconceived notions of Black under-achievement, serves as a beacon for Black children and young people. It will contribute to overcoming Black underachievement by motivating pupils.

Focusing on the successes of other Black people who have come through the British educational system successfully and achieved academically can be as effective a motivator as an encouraging teacher or parent. It is time to recognise such achievements on the one hand, while challenging racism and underachievement on the other.

Conclusion

Unless all these agencies coordinate their efforts, it is unlikely that much will change. *Tell it Like it is: How our schools fail Black children* was published in 2005. It contains Bernard Coard's analysis from 1971: *How the West Indian Child is made Educationally Subnormal in the British School System.* The accompanying writings of academics and activists show that little has changed in terms of Black educational achievement since the original publication of Coard's influential book.

My research has highlighted several issues that warrant further research. One is informal exclusion, where pupils are sent out of class for a period longer than a day or sent home informally. Informal exclusion is on the increase; it needs to be formally documented and researched and the implications for pupils' progress in school explored.

Although aware of the limitations of my study – a snapshot conducted within a limited time, under particular circumstances and with particular individuals, some of them atypical – it throws new light on the experiences of Black children in the UK. Its analysis of their learning experiences has established that the home and the community are crucial to the development of resilience and high achievement. Importantly it shows that government, local authorities and schools which are ultimately responsible for education need to recognise that once ethnic minority pupils are given true equality of opportunity to achieve within the education system, academic standards will be raised for all pupils. This research challenges those who interact with Black children at all levels to work to create positive environments that will enable eagles to soar.

Bibliography

Appiah, L. (2002) London Schools and the Black child: towards a vision of excellence. *Multicultural Teaching* 20 (3) 6-12

Blair, M. (1994) Black teachers Black students and education markets. *Cambridge Journal of Education*, 24, p277-291

Blair, M. (2001) *Why Pick on Me?* Stoke on Trent: Trentham Books

Blair, M. and Bourne, J. (1998) *Making the Difference Teaching and Learning in Successful Multi-Ethnic Schools*. London: DfEE

Blyth, E. and Milner, J. (1993) 'Exclusion from school: A first step in exclusion from society'? *Children and Society*, 7:3, 255-268.

Brierley, P. (2006) *Religious Trends*. London: Christian Research

Bronfenbrenner, U. (1979) *The Ecology of Human Development: Experiments by Nature and Design*. Cambridge, Massachusetts: Harvard University Press

Channer, Y. (1995) *I Am A Promise: The School Achievement of British African-Caribbeans*. Stoke on Trent: Trentham Books

Cline, T., de Abreu, G., Fihosy, C., Gray, H., Lambert, H. and Neale, J. (2002) *Minority Ethnic Pupils in Mainly White Schools*. DFES

Coard, B. (1971) *How the West Indian Child is made Educationally subnormal in the British School System*. London: New Beacon

Commission for Racial Equality (1996) *Exclusion from School: The Public Cost*. London: Belmont Press.

Commission for Racial Equality (1997) *Ethnic Minority Women*. London: CRE Factsheet

Crozier, G. (1996) Black Parents and School Relationships: A Case Study. *Educational Review*, 48:3, 253-267

Crozier, G. (2001) Excluded Parents: The De-racialisation of Parental Involvement [1] *Race Ethnicity and Education*, 4:4, 329-341

DfEE (2000) *Removing the Barriers: Raising Achievement Levels of Minority Ethnic Pupils. Key Points for Schools*. DFEE 0012/0000

DfES (2003) *Aiming High: Raising the Achievement of Minority Ethnic Pupils*. DFES/0183/2003

DfES (2006) *National Curriculum Assessment, GCSE and equivalent attainment and post 16 attainment by pupil characteristics in England 2005.* First Release 09/2006

Eggleston, J., Dunn, D. and Anjali, M. (1986) *Education for Some: the educational and vocational experiences of 15-18 year old members of ethnic minority groups.* Stoke on Trent: Trentham Books

Fife-Schaw, C. (1995) Questionnaire Design In G. Breackwell, S. Hammond, and C. Fife-Schaw (eds.) *Research Methods in Psychology* London: Sage

Fuller, M. (1980) 'Black Girls in a London Comprehensive'. In M. Hammersley and P. Woods (eds.), *Life in School: The Sociology of Pupil Culture.* Milton Keynes: OUP.

Gaine, C. and George, R. (1999) *Gender, 'Race' and Class in Schooling: A New Introduction.* London: Falmer Press

Gillborn, D. (1990) *Race, Ethnicity and Education.* London: Unwin Hyman

Gillborn, D. (2001) Racism, policy and the (mis)-education of Black children. In R. Major (ed.) *Educating Our Black Children: New Directions and Radical Approaches.* London: Routledge Falmer

Gillborn, D. (2002) *Education and Institutional Racism.* London: Institute of Education, University of London

Gillborn, D. And Gipps, C. (1996) *Recent Research on the Achievements of Ethnic Minority Pupils.* London: HMSO.

Gillborn, D. and Mirza, H. (2000) *Educational Inequality: Mapping Race, Class and Gender: A Synthesis of Research Evidence.* London: Ofsted.

Gillborn, D. and Youdell, D. (2000) *Rationing Education: Policy, Practice, Reform and Equity.* Buckingham: OUP

Haight, W.L. (2002) *African-American Children at Church: A Socio-cultural Perspective.* Cambridge: Cambridge University Press.

Hamilton, D. and Rose, R. (1980) Illusory correlation and the maintenance of stereotypic beliefs. *Journal of Personality and Social Psychology,* 39, p1050-63

Hildago, M., Siu, S., Bright, J., Swap, S. and Epstein, J. (1995) Research on families, schools and communities: a multicultural perspective. In J. Banks and C. Banks (eds) *Handbook of Research on Multicultural Education.* New York: Macmillian

Lee, V. E., Winfield, L. F. and Wilson, T. C. (1991) Academic behaviours among high achieving African American students. *Education and Urban Society,* 24:1, 65-86

MacDonald, J. (2001) *Portraits of Black Achievement: Composing Successful Careers.* Trowbridge: Lifetime Careers Publishing

Macpherson, W. (1999) *The Stephen Lawrence Inquiry Report.* London: CRE

Majors, R. (Ed.) (2001) *Educating Our Black Children.* London: Routledge Falmer.

Mackinnon, D., Statham, J and Hales, M. (1995) *Education in the UK: Facts and Figures.* London: Hodder and Stoughton

Mirza, H. (1992) *Young, Female and Black.* London: Routledge

Modood, T., Berthoud, R., Lakey, J., Nazroo, J., Smith, P., Virdee, S. and Beishon, S. (1997) *Diversity and Disadvantage: Ethnic Minorities in Britain.* London: Policy Studies Institute

Morse, J.M. (1994) Designing funded Qualitative Research. In N.K. Denzin and Y.S. Lincoln, *The Handbook of Qualitative Research.* Thousand Oaks, California: Sage

Nehaul, K. (1996) *The Schooling of Children of Caribbean Heritage.* Stoke on Trent: Trentham Books.

Nettles, S. M. (1991) 'Community contributions to school outcomes of African-American students.' *Education and Urban Society,* 24:1,132-147

Ofsted, (1996) *Exclusions From Secondary Schools.* London: HMSO

Ofsted (1999) *Raising the Achievement of Minority Ethnic Pupils: School and LEA Responses.* London: HMSO

Ofsted (2001a) *Managing Support for the Attainment of Pupils from Minority Ethnic Groups.* London: HMSO

Osler, A. (1997b) *Exclusion From School and Racial Equality.* London: CRE.

Osler, A. (1997c) *The Education and Careers of Black Teachers.* Buckingham: Open University Press.

Osler, A., Watling, R., Busher, H., Cole, T., and White, A. (2001) *Reasons for Exclusion From School.* London: DfEE

Owen, D., Green, A., Pitcher, J., and Maguire, (2000) *Race Research for the Future: Minority Ethnic Participation and Achievements in Education, Training and the Labour Market.* London. DfEE Research Brief No. 225.

Parsons, C., Hayden, C., Godfrey, R., Howlett, K., and Martin, T. (2001) *Outcomes in Secondary Education For Children Excluded From Primary School.* London: DfEE

Pollard, D.S. (1989) Against the Odds: A profile of academic achievers from the urban underclass. *Journal of Negro Education,* 58 , 297-308.

Rampton, B. (1995) *Crossing: Language and Ethnicity among adolescents.* London: Longman

Richman, J.M. and Bowen, G. L. (1997) School Failure: An Ecological-Inter-actional-Development Perspective. In M. R Fraser (ed) *Risk and Resilience in Childhood: An Ecological Perspective.* Washington: NatashaSW Press

Rhamie, J. and Hallam, S. (2002) An Investigation into African-Caribbean Academic Success in the UK. *Race Ethnicity and Education,* 5:2, 151-170

Richardson, B. (Ed.) (2005) *Tell it like it is: How Our Schools Fail Black Children.* Stoke on Trent: Trentham Books and Bookmarks

Richardson, R. and Wood, A. (1999) *Inclusive Schools Inclusive Society: race and identity on the agenda.* Stoke on Trent: Trentham Books

Robson, C. (2002) *Real World Research.* Oxford: Blackwell

Rutter, M. (1987) Psychosocial Resilience and Protective Mechanisms. *American Journal of Orthopsychiatry*, 53: 3

Schunck, D. (1987) Self efficacy and motivated learning. In N. Hastings and J. Schwieso (eds) *New Directions in educational Psychology*. London: Falmer Press

Sewell, T. (1997) *Black Masculinities and Schooling*. Stoke on Trent: Trentham Books.

Sewell, T. (2000) Beyond Institutional racism: tackling the real problems of Black underachievement. *Multicultural Teaching*, 18:2, 27-33

Simon, D. (2005) Education of the Blacks: the supplementary school movement in B.Richardson (Ed.) *Tell it like it is: How our schools fail Black children*. Stoke on Trent: Trentham Books and Bookmarks

Tajfel, H. (Ed.) (1978) *Differentiation between Social Groups: Studies in the Social Psychology of Inter-group Relations*. London: Academic Press

Taylor M. (1981) *Caught Between: A Review of Research into the Education of Pupils of West Indian Origin*. Windsor: NFER-Nelson.

The Black Child Report (1999-2000) London: Peoplescience Intelligence Unit.

Tizard, B., Blatchford, P., Burke, J., Farquhar, C. and Plewis, I. (1988) *Young Children at School in the Inner City*. London: Routledge

Tomlin, C. (2006) An Analysis of High Attaining Black Students: Factors and Conditions that Affect their Achievement Levels. University of Wolverhampton: www. Multiverse.ac.uk

Tomlinson, S. (1983) Black Women in Higher Education – case studies of university women in Britain. In L. Barton and S. Walker, *Race Class and Education*. London: Croom Helm

Tomlinson, S. (1986) *Ethnic Minority Achievement and Equality of Opportunity*. University of Nottingham: School of Education

Troyna, B. (1984) ' Fact or Artefact? The educational underachievement 'of black pupils, *British Journal of Sociology of Education*, 5 (2) p 153-160.

Upton, G. and Cooper, P. (1991) A new perspective on behaviour problems in schools: The Ecosystemic Approach. *Maladjustment and Therapeutic Education*, 8, 1

Wrench, J. and Hassan, E. (1996) *Ambition and Marginalisation: A Qualitative study of Underachieving Young Men of Afro-Caribbean Origin*. DFEE Research Series No. 31. London: DFEE

Wright, C. (1988) The school experience of pupils of West Indian background. Unpublished PhD thesis, University of Keele quoted in Y. Channer (1995) *I Am A Promise*. Stoke on Trent: Trentham Books.

Wright, C. (1992) *Race Relations in the Primary School*. London: David Fulton

Yan, W. (1999) 'Successful African American Students: The Role of Parental Involvement'. *Journal of Negro Education*, 68:15-22

Index